CHOOSING TO LIFT EVERY VOICE AND SING

A Series of Faith-Based and Patriotic Mini-Seminars
For Teaching and Mentoring African American Youth
(and Their Friends of All Races)

ELIZABETH BRANCH, EdD

To order additional copies of this book, contact:
Xlibris
844-714-8691
www.Xlibris.com
Orders@Xlibris.com

ISBN: Softcover   978-1-6698-2562-3
         Hardcover   978-1-6698-2563-0
         EBook   978-1-6698-2561-6

Print information available on the last page

Rev. date: 08/03/2022

CHOOSING TO LIFT EVERY VOICE and SING

A Series of Faith-Based and Patriotic Mini-Seminars for Teaching A KEEPSAKE and Mentoring African American Youth (and Their Friends Of All Races)

Elizabeth Branch, EdD, Author

Contributing Writers: Jokwon J. Bagby, MA
Jamese M. Branch, BA

Contents

About the Author

Dr. Elizabeth Grady Branch is a proud mother, grandmother, educator and a faith-based author.

Born into abject poverty in deep East Texas, she graduated from the segregated Fred Douglass High school in Jacksonville. She received a Bachelor's degree in Elementary Education, from Jarvis Christian College (now University), a Master's from Texas Southern University, and a Doctorate of Education from North Texas State University (now University of North Texas). Her job and career experiences spanned the gamut. Standouts included migrant cotton picker, waitressing, seasonal field worker and other menial jobs to help the family income. However, her career after college included the joys and rewards of becoming a K-College level teacher, administrator, and small business owner.

Having been blessed with such a wide range of successful experiences, plus living and thriving thru the part of American history known as "Jim Crow" and the Civil Rights Movement, makes her a highly qualified contender to promote this agenda. It is designed to instill pride, faith, "personal nobility", love, and hope in the youth of color in our country, America.

Her curriculum materials and "old school" wisdom gained from her past are applicable today.

With A Contributing Team of Readers/Consultants:

Jeanette Adkins/ Author, College English Professor

Stephanie Arceneaux/ High School Counselor, Administrator

Marcus LeeForrest Branch/ Business Owner, Cartoonist

Dr. Lisa Bryant, Minister/ Counselor

Lola Mae Campbell/ Retired Teacher

Dorothy Davis/ Retired College Reading Instructor

Pharoah Davis/ Artist, Author, Activist

Opal Grady Garrett/ Retired Teacher, Business Owner

Sandy Baker Grady/ Vice Principal

Dr. Cheryl Harris/ Retired College Administrator

Audrey Hatley/ Dyslexic Reading Specialist

Kymberly Keeton/ Art Librarian

Dr. Arthur Lyn Morgan/ Principal

Bethanye Branch Morgan/ College Professor

Deyonne Primo/ CEO Daughters, Inc.

Dr. Shewanda Riley/ Author, College English Professor

Teacher/Leader/Caring Adult TRAINING Notes:

This section is offered to help enlighten, promote, and ease the task of the mini-seminar leader(s) as much as possible. Teaching and learning the lyrics of this special song, Lift Every Voice and Sing, could be done with a sheet of paper, time set aside for reading it, and memorization of the lyrics. However, suggestions will be offered throughout, to help each mini-seminar leader to walk away with much more than having presented a routine "book lesson" for this keepsake.

There are faith-based history lessons, interactive sessions, literacy enhancing activities, up-to-date discussion topics, takeaways, musical videos, and much more! Look for basic literacy skills involving reading, writing, spelling, thinking, speaking, phonics, following directions, and more academic support is included. Color coding is used to help direct and manage the activities better. Practical pre/post surveys, answer keys and other teaching tools are in the appendix. Planning ahead is most effective. We encourage and demonstrate polite thought-provoking discussions...no interruptions, waiting turns, one at a time, etc.

The leaders (and participants) will come away with knowing the lyrics, patriotic meanings, and helpful memories that will continue to linger long after the sessions have ended. The opportunity to instill more love, hope, pride, and joy to fellow Americans, regardless of color, should not be taken lightly. It's as important today as it was in the past. Share as many of the lessons as are needed.

By all means, teach and lead the program in your own faith-based creative way. However, with this training, additional supplemental instructional materials, and these suggestions, you are even more prepared and equipped to enjoy "LIFT EVERY VOICE AND SING..., IT'S YOUR CHOICE!"

Special TRAINING NOTE About the Intent and Mission:

Our intent is to offer 15 faith-based mini-seminars designed to be used as supplemental instructional materials for teaching the lyrics in Lift Every Voice and Sing.

Even now, as we approach the semisesquintennial, 250-year celebration, many Americans, young and old, are hurt, embarrassed, mad, disappointed, insecure, and feel that justice IS denied, due to skin color. It is a mental, social and emotional burden that challenges our very being. But faith and hope is still alive and knowing a Creator in our midst is the Balm we need! Read the news, observe what is happening, become aware of our surroundings and the statistics will become a reality. As Believers, leaders and caring adults, we do not have all of the answers or solutions. But we cannot pretend or ignore facts. So, my pastor, Maverick Gayden reminds us often, "if you see something, do something" …until something better comes along is our charge as Believers. Our intent, or "something", is to build from the inside… a "personal nobility", "an individual virtue", and/or a sense of pride. We must listen and help those that are abused understand the dynamics that feed into the racist and bigoted behaviors directed toward them in a safe and supportive environment. We want young people to choose to feel better about themselves because they know they are God's creation. We must help victims to choose to want to rise above the ugliness and move forward, as many of our ancestors did, in spite of the circumstances.

These 15 amazing interactive lessons in each mini-seminar utilize

1. Historical Topics to Prompt Listening, Thinking, and Discussion
2. Musical and Performance Videos for Instruction and Entertainment
3. Literacy-Based Group Interactive Learning Activities

Our mission is

- to help heal some of the social emotional pains of racism experienced by many African Americans!
- to help understand and prepare for patriotic celebrations, camps, and events (Juneteenth, Veterans Day, Independence Day, Black History Month, Semiquincentennial and other African American events and patriotic celebrations)!
- to instill racial heritage pride in African American youth!
- to share our unique American history with families and friends of all colors!
- to learn the lyrics and lift our voices in appreciation of a tangible keepsake from our unique heritage, Lift Every Voice and Sing!

Special TRAINING NOTE About <u>Suggested</u> Methodology:

<u>SUGGESTED</u> MINI-SEMINAR STRATEGIES:

Good and effective teachers, mentors, and leaders will possess a variety of teaching techniques to be used at their disposal during their mini-seminars. They know that they are likely to have varied learners, different learning styles, multiple backgrounds, interest/grade levels, and degrees of involvement in each seminar. After training, they should use whatever they are most comfortable with for the audience at the time. Remember, there are very few right or wrong answers in this type of mini-seminar. We want participants to learn from honest, polite, open conversation. We encourage participants to discuss (talk), interact (share), and communicate their thoughts and feelings. To make this happen, the trained leaders (teachers, mentors, etc.) must become thoroughly familiar with the seminar materials and structure. Participatory ground rules must be established ahead of time. The truth and facts, lived experiences are expected,... not biased opinions. Leaders must attempt to take time to listen and place value on each child. A preferred strategy is that leaders should know the material so well, they can plan to be flexible in the delivery of instructions. Opportunities for positive and faith-based feedback, repetition of information, and words of encouragement for each participant will yield better results. A <u>suggestion</u> to each leader is to add, subtract, and/or create teaching/learning strategies that will work for the good of every learner.

Each portion of the mini-seminars, has purpose in helping participants to embrace a culture and the keepsake, Lift Every Voice ...

A Special TRAINING NOTE About <u>Suggested</u> Teaching Steps:

The 15 mini-seminars are organized in the same format for each lesson, mostly. Each is designed to introduce topics of interest to help participants understand why our unique ancestral presence can and should be celebrated.

Step 1 is the pre-test/survey. It is given only once before instructions begin. It is suggested (and important) so that the leader, as well as the learner, can see where they are starting in their thinking and understanding prior to the mini-seminars. (The pre/post surveys are located in the Appendix)

Step 2 includes all of the chosen methods of teaching the formal, informal, personal and interactive learning activities. It is the main portion of the mini-seminars activities.

Step 3 is the post-test/survey. It is designed to see what measurable differences have occurred since the start of the mini-seminars.

Here is a summary of the lesson steps. None are carved in stone, but they have proven to be effective in their delivery in the past.

(NOTE: CARING ADULTS WILL ALWAYS BE AVAILABLE IF NEEDED!)

Step 1. PRE-TEST/SURVEY (Only Once Before Lessons Begin)

Step 2. TEACHING STRATEGIES FOR MINI-SEMINARS

- <u>READ/DISCUSS</u> INTRODUCTIONS and MOTIVATIONAL MOMENTS
- <u>DISCUSS</u> "SHOUT-OUT"/TRIBUTE TO ANCESTOR
- <u>HUDDLE</u> FOR ENCOURAGEMENT & DIRECTIONS
- <u>VIEW</u> VIDEO/DISCUSS
- <u>ENGAGE/DISCUSS</u> IN GROUP ACTIVITIES
- <u>LISTEN /DISCUSS</u> LEADER'S "see it! fix it! disown it! ", UPDATE/TAKEAWAYS

Step 3. POST- TEST/SURVEY (Given at the conclusion of seminars)

A Special TRAINING NOTE About the Cover To Share:

Augusta Savage was a famous Harlem Renaissance artist, activist, and educator. Her reputation as an outstanding sculptor was well known throughout the country. In spite of this dark time of America's history, Ms. Savage was commissioned to provide a sculpture at the 1939 World's Fair. As a result, she created and presented The Harp. Her work was, as expected, amazing! It was said to have been an extraordinary piece of work that stood 16 feet high. She sculpted 12 stylized young black singers dressed in choir robes of graduated heights shaped in the form of a harp. The composition cast the singers as instruments of God. The sculpture stood in a prominent place near one of the entrances to the fair. Over 5 million visitors viewed her work. It was very popular and well received by all. Lift Every Voice and Sing was written as a poem by James Weldon Johnson in the latter 1800s and it was set to music by his brother, John Rosamond Johnson. They were friends of Savage. She wanted to name her sculpture in honor of Lift Every Voice and Sing and what it represented. It was not allowed. Instead, she settled for The HARP. Unfortunately, at the end of the fair, the piece was demolished. The money needed to cast it in bronze and store it was not allocated in the budget. However, her work was captured in the hearts of many, then and now.

Choose to concentrate on her inborn talents and self-taught skills. She was not "university" trained. God created her with the innate ability to produce this type of work prior to a formal education. Equally as important, He created her to have a passion for her work and an appreciation of others as well. Participants should know that this woman and her ancestors were considered, by many, to be less than human because of skin color. Lift Every Voice and Sing and the Harp demonstrates why Africans forced to become a part of the American dream can do so proudly! We can and must be, as survivors and thrivers, proud of such a unique legacy! Choose to share it!

SECTION 1.

MINI - SEMINARS 1-5

SEMINAR 1. LIFT EVERY VOICE AND SING, AN AMAZING SONG OF FAITH AND HOPE IN GOD AND IN AMERICA!

I. INTRODUCTION: In this listening/learning session, we will explore reasons many of our people of color embrace these lyrics. Lift Every Voice and Sing is a national representation and tribute to our unique African American heritage. These lyrics encouraged our ancestors to imagine a new day filled with great rejoicing and the blessed sounds of freedom and liberty! Many audiences sing only one verse, but there are three beautiful faith-based stanzas that are filled with words of encouragement, direction, resiliency, wisdom, pride, and hope! Despite the adversities they faced and endured in bondage, our ancestors were encouraged to keep moving forward. You can choose to keep moving forward as well! This song of faith in God and hope in America is timeless and practical. Choose to embrace it, proudly, and teach it to others. It is a precious keepsake from our African American past and heritage.

II. MOTIVATIONAL MOMENT: In 1899, a great poet, James Weldon Johnson and his brother, a classical musician, John Rosamond Johnson wrote an amazing song about an amazing group of Americans! They were the descendants of Black Africans captured and brought to America to be placed in enslavement. Centuries later, this shameful and immoral system was to have been abolished through patriotic laws and actions of people in power. But a land claiming to offer freedom, after over 200 years of FREE labor, made this a difficult choice to accept and obey. For many landowners, even when they knew slavery had become illegal and wrong, they were hesitant and derelict in keeping these laws and promises. Many whites gained multigenerational wealth and power during this time. Black people, however, suffered horrendously. Most had no land nor startup resources, but they refused to give up. They worked wherever and tried to survive without due and promised laws of support and protection. Lynching, burnings and other acts and threats of violence from the Ku Klux Klan, and other white supremacist groups were ongoing. Many white citizens, clergy, policemen and law enforcement did little or nothing to prevent these acts of terrorism. In fact, many in this group were perpetrators. Blacks naturally developed a fear and distrust for law enforcement. Yet, during one of the darkest hours from our past, this poet, songwriter, and his brother tried to share hope through this song. It is an amazing treasure and keepsake! Today, we realize we have inherited a great nation as descendants of a great people. Our fore parents invested in our future in America through their struggles and sacrifices of much blood, sweat and tears. Their faith in God was strong! They were strong! They chose to keep going forward! They never gave up! Choose to be proud of them! They bore a high sacrificial cost for us. Through many "weary" years they help to build America into a great nation. It was an investment in you and your opportunities in this great country! Now, as we prepare to celebrate the Semiquincentennial in 2026, we want you to stand proudly! Choose to enjoy the privileges of a land of freedom to worship, raise a family, and enjoy the fruits of careers and educational opportunities! Our ancestors wanted that for you! Today, we can proudly lift our voices and remind all that can hear, we stand on the shoulders of these strong, intelligent, talented, and courageous faith-based giants. WE OWE IT TO THEM! YOU CAN CHOOSE TO BE EXTREMELY PROUD OF THEIR SACRIFICES! There is NO reason for shame, bitterness, nor defeat. Hold your head high and "lift your voice and sing, till earth and heaven ring!" It's YOUR CHOICE!

III. DISCUSSION/LISTENING SESSION: A "SHOUT OUT" AND TRIBUTE TO OUR ANSCESTORS? WHY? WHY NOT?

IV. #1/GROUP ACTIVITIES: AN AMAZING SONG FOR AN AMAZING PEOPLE!

A. HUDDLE: Participants in this program are being introduced to an amazing gift and keepsake. To learn the lyrics of this song will offer a gift that keeps on giving spiritually, socially, and academically. It is a song of faith and hope in God and in America's promises. Many audiences sing only one verse, but there are three beautiful stanzas filled with words of resiliency, wisdom, direction, pride and joyous hope! Written years ago, 1899, by James W. and John R. Johnson (two brothers), the lyrics are timeless, and they are still practical and useful.

B. SPECIAL ACTIVITIES/DISCUSSION/ASK YOUR LEADER FOR HELP IF NEEDED.

Activity 1. GOOGLE VIDEO: JADA HOLLIDAY, Baylor University, Lift Every Voice and Sing. Please listen and observe for discussion.

Activity 2. Your leader will introduce each line of the stanzas. Place a check in front of each line introduced. Double check lines needing more review.

___Lift Every Voice and Sing, Till earth and Heaven ring
___Ring with the harmony of Liberty,
___Let our rejoicing rise, High as the list'ning skies,
___Let it resound loud as the rolling seas,
___Sing a song, full of the faith that our dark past has taught us,
___Sing a song, full of the hope that the present has brought us,
___Facing a rising song, of our new day begun, Let us march on till victory is won!

___Stony the road we trod, bitter the chast'ning rod,
___Felt in the days when hope unborn had died,
___Yet with a steady beat, Have not our weary feet
___Come to a place for which our fathers sighed?
___We have come, over a way that with tears has been watered,
___We have come, treading our path through the blood of the slaughtered,
___Out from the gloomy past, Till now we stand at last, Where the white gleam of our bright star is cast.
___God of our weary years, God of our silent tears,
___Thou who has brought us thus far on the way
___Though who has by thou might, led us into the light,
___Keep us forever in the right path we pray,
___Lest our feet stray from the places, our God where we met Thee
___Lest our hearts drunk with the wine of the world we forget Thee
___Shadowed beneath Thy hand, May we forever stand,
True to our God, True to our Native land.

Activity 3. GIVE ORAL RESPONSES FOR THE BLANKS:

Last names of the Author(s) _____, Year written? _____, One major purpose was to give _____. In researching the word 'Semiquincentennial', which part means five (5) or fifty (50) _____? How old will you be in the year of the 250th celebration? ____

V. #1/DISCUSSION: "SEE IT! FIX IT! DISOWN IT!" TAKEAWAYS!: Your leader will display these selected articles from BUZZFEED, by Morgan Sloss... "Black People Are Sharing The Rules They Follow That Most White People Don't Even Know About, And This Is So Important "(Goodful, Posted on April 27, 2022).

Seminar 1. "My mother taught me to ALWAYS ask for a bag and receipt, no matter how small the purchase, or you can be accused of stealing" ___Anonymous

I Choose to AGREE with this advice! WHY?

_____

_____

I Choose to DISAGREE with this advice! WHY?

_____

_____

I Choose to ABSTAIN at this time! WHY?

_____

_____

CAN YOU SHARE SIMILAR "rules" YOU HAVE IMPLEMENTED PERSONALLY? ADVICE?

_____

_____

GROUP SUMMARY ACTIVITY:

"Our CHOICES for this "American" story are to 1) "see it" (admit it's existence); 2)"fix it" (work to eradicate); or 3) "disown it" (ignore its presence). As faith-based Americans, whose ancestors faced similar or worse adversities, which is your choice? WHY? Write your group's choice and discussion notes on the following page.

Our CHOICE for this story is_____.

Why is this important discussion for Americans who are Believers today? These rules evolve from stereotyping, prejudices, and unfair thoughts about people of color. They are mentally and emotionally stressful for the majority of Black Americans. Yet, they are not likely to go away soon. So, the discussions can provide useful takeaways for peace loving, non-confrontational, and law-abiding citizens. Contrary to racist views, many African Americans still look for positive approaches to solving prolonged injustices in a civil, self-empowering, and faith-based manner. Some of these "rules", if not handled properly, even today, can be life altering or worse. Discuss possible ways we can improve and maintain our freedom loving lives while avoiding more mental and emotional stress. Choose to be proud of the unique heritage of strength, patience, love, dignity, and honor modeled by our ancestors, in the face of adversity. Some of these "rules" were a part of their lives, too. **PREPARE TO SHARE!**

NOTES:

_____

_____

_____

_____

_____

_____

_____

_____

_____

_____

_____

_____

_____

SEMINAR 2. LIFT EVERY VOICE AND SING, TILL IT RINGS WITH THE HARMONIES OF LIBERTY FOR ALL AMERICANS, REGARDLESS OF RACE, CREED, OR COLOR!

I. INTRODUCTION: In this lesson, we will continue to explore more reasons many people of color, and some white citizens, embraced these inspiring lyrics in Lift Every Voice and Sing. Even though it was written during a wrenching and turbulent time of the late 1800's, both races of Believers, included this song in their congregational churches' hymnals. Black and white Americans knew its potential to promote unity, inspiration, faith, and hope. They knew that America, lawfully and unlawfully, had failed to keep its promises to our ancestors. It was truly amazing that "out from [such] a gloomy past" there could be such displays of faith, hope, and forgiveness as felt in these lyrics. Our ancestors welcomed the support shown from their fellow white believers. You can choose to be proud of such a strong blessed faith-based and forgiving response. It's a natural and important part of your heritage! Be proud! It is your choice!

II. MOTIVATIONAL MOMENTS: Do you ever think about how difficult life must have been for your parents, grandparents, and/or great-grandparents because of their race? Their ancestors faced even more challenging times. Talk to "old people" sometimes. Take time to listen to their stories from their past. You will, proudly, discover how determined our people were to SURVIVE, THRIVE, and TO LEAD...EVEN FROM BEHIND! Most times their situations in life were not ideal, desired, or desirable! But many made the choice to keep moving forward. And they never gave up hope despite overt and covert cruel inequities. For many "weary" times over the years, it appeared to be a hopeless lonely journey. But many of our ancestors fought, successfully, for creative, civil, political, and constructive faith-based ways to help solve America's racial problems. Fortunately, their efforts have always been assisted by small faith-based groups of all races, along the way. Unfortunately, a lot of true historical facts, occurrences, and interesting events were not taught in positive settings. Topics concerning the worth, value, and contributions to make you proud and help you to understand your African American heritage were not always emphasized or discussed. The ever present need to fight poverty and gain voting power, is an example. Did white Americans always fight to keep us down? NO! Many fair and lawful attempts were promised and made to make America a land of freedom for all her people. White Christians, abolitionists, and freedom loving sympathizers tried to help. Many Whites held some Blacks in high esteem and helped to establish schools, churches, organizations, positions of authority, etc., but they were challenged by cruel mean-spirited racist bigots, too. Some knew that they were evil, some didn't quite understand or care, and most, but not all, tried to hide it. Many were bullies who wore sheets to cover their identity or for security purposes. Our skin color, however, couldn't be hidden. We were easily targeted and became victims of despicable and unequivocal racial and sexual torture and discrimination. Back then, our skin color was the dominant focal point of most of the divisiveness and racial injustices in America, NOT women or LGBTQs. For instance, there were NO water fountains, NO cafes or eating establishments, NO libraries, NO parks, NO Sundown towns, etc. with signs prohibiting these groups. Yet, there were plenty aimed at people of color...SOMETIMES, from members of THIS VERY GROUP! No other law-abiding American citizens, as a marginalized group, endured the displays of open hostilities as those directed at our African American fore parents. Yet, though many died, many survived. They thrived! They chose to continue to help America live up to its promises. They, along with other races in America, did not give up! You must choose NOT to give up! Choose to continue to "rise and build." Choose to lift your voices and sing!

III. DISCUSSION/LISTENING SESSION: A "SHOUT OUT" AND TRIBUTE TO MY ANSCESTORS? WHY? WHY NOT?

IV. #2/GROUP ACTIVITIES
LIFT EVERY VOICE AND SING...WE OWE IT TO OURSELVES AND OUR ANCESTORS!

A. HUDDLE: Slavery, peonage, segregation, black codes, Jim Crow, prison and an unjust racist governmental system would have caused many to give up. But even though our ancestors were challenged, over the centuries, they held on tenaciously. They continued to fight and won the freedoms we enjoy today. When our nation is unified, there is none greater on earth! As we approach the big Semiquincentennial celebration, let us all help lift America up! You must choose to never give up! "Fight now and "till victory is won!" "Who will speak for America...?" You can! "Who will tell our story...?" You can! It's in your DNA! YOU CAN CHOOSE TO BE PROUD!

B. SPECIAL ACTIVITIES: (Always ask your leader for help if you need it)

Activity 1. Google each of the suggested short videos below. If you could share only one version of the three presentations with a mentee, which would you choose 1st, 2nd, and 3rd? Why? Think critically and be prepared to defend your choice.

___ Conwell Choir, Mark Asch, Lift Every Voice and Sing

___Oak Wood Alumni Committed Singers, Lift Every Voice and Sing

___Chicago Children's Choir, Lift Every Voice and Sing

Arrange and write them in your order of priority.

1st _____

2nd _____

3rd _____

Activity 2. Browse the internet in the time allotted for more versions of Lift Every Voice and Sing. Look at Beyonce, Aretha Franklin, OR, find at least one other version you would like to share with the class. Why is this one of most interest to you? Think critically and list your choice here.

Name_____ Length of Time_____

Notes of defense _____

_____

_____

V. #2/DISCUSSION: "SEE IT! FIX IT! DISOWN IT!" TAKEAWAYS!: Your leader will display these selected articles from BUZZFEED, by Morgan Sloss... "Black People Are Sharing The Rules They Follow That Most White People Don't Even Know About, And This Is So Important "(Goodful, Posted on April 27, 2022).

Seminar 2. "I'm from Louisiana where they still have 'sundown towns'. Avoid them at all costs, but if you have to pass through at night, MAKE SURE YOU HAVE A FULL TANK OF GAS so that you don't have to stop". ____bigscooby04

I Choose to AGREE with this advice! WHY?

_____

_____

I Choose to DISAGREE with this advice! WHY?

_____

_____

I Choose to ABSTAIN at this time! WHY?

_____

_____

CAN YOU SHARE SIMILAR "rules" YOU HAVE IMPLEMENTED PERSONALLY? ADVICE?

_____

_____

GROUP SUMMARY ACTIVITY:

"Our CHOICES for this "American" story are to 1) "see it" (admit it's existence); 2)"fix it" (work to eradicate); or 3) "disown it" (ignore its presence). As faith-based Americans, whose ancestors faced similar or worse adversities, which is your choice? WHY? Write your group's choice and discussion notes on the following page.

Our CHOICE for this story is _____.

Why is this important discussion for Americans who are Believers today? These rules evolve from stereotyping, prejudices, and unfair thoughts about people of color. They are mentally and emotionally stressful for the majority of Black Americans. Yet, they are not likely to go away soon. So, the discussions can provide useful takeaways for peace loving, non-confrontational, and law-abiding citizens. Contrary to racist views, many African Americans still look for positive approaches to solving prolonged injustices in a civil, self-empowering, and faith-based manner. Some of these "rules", if not handled properly, even today, can be life altering or worse. Discuss possible ways we can improve and maintain our freedom loving lives while avoiding more mental and emotional stress. Choose to be proud of the unique heritage of strength, patience, love, dignity, and honor modeled by our ancestors, in the face of adversity. Some of these "rules" were a part of their lives, too. **PREPARE TO SHARE!**

NOTES:

_____

_____

_____

_____

_____

_____

_____

_____

_____

_____

_____

_____

SEMINAR 3. LIFT EVERY VOICE AND SING: WE CAN CHOOSE TO SING A PATRIOTIC SONG!

I. INTRODUCTION: Sometimes, it is difficult to think of America as our home given the obstacles most African Americans have faced in our past. But, whether we, or someone else, have a problem with the fact, this is our home. And WE can choose to help make it into a pleasant home or a chaotic one. MOST SUCCESSFUL CITIZENS have chosen to "be better, not bitter" and unafraid. There is no one way we can diminish, erase, or pretend the harsh realities of the pain and suffering and negative experiences racism and racist practices have caused. There is NO one way to "rise and build," but you must choose to make the latter happen. You can choose! Honor your noble heritage and for your own future, choose to become "more than a conqueror" and win! Winning is your reward! Choose to "RISE and BUILD" TOWARD YOUR AMAZING SUCCESS IN AMERICA! It is a choice you can experience and make!

II. MOTIVATIONAL MOMENTS: Our history dictates WE ARE THE ONLY GROUP OF CITIZENS FORCED TO BECOME AMERICANS! Our ancestors were kidnapped, captured and stolen en masse to build America. Through our fore parents' continuous FREE labor, we helped to build a great nation. We were not paid, treated fairly or equally for many centuries. Meanwhile, many white farmers, plantation owners, and land holders prospered using our ancestors as their free workforce. They developed and acquired generational wealth for their families...then and today. Whether free or in enslavement, our fore parents' contributions were invaluable and needed by this young developing country. Though extremely challenging, our love and faith in God taught us how to continue to love America, to nurture and believe in her, despite the adversities we faced. We, too, bought into the promises of what true FREEDOM could offer us in an America strong enough to rid itself of a racist unequal system of government. Our ancestors trusted America to stay true to its promises to us and all its citizens. Fredrick Douglass, Martin Luther King, Sr., Mary McLeod Bethune, Josephine Ruffin, Ida B. Wells, and many others had the ear of powerful white people in their era. They knew that more unity meant more progress. Blacks and whites, united for America's progress in many ways. Mary W. Ovington, Andrew Carnegie, Joan Zitzelman, Susan B. Anthony, John Rockefeller and many other whites were supportive. Together, they formed organizations, supplied funds, contributed to acts of valor that encouraged Americans, and America, to keep its promises to all its people, regardless of skin color. The Niagara Movement, NAACP, National Association of Colored Women's Clubs, and the National Urban League are only a few organizations started by Blacks and whites working in unity. They all dreamed and continued to work for equality. Now, as we approach the Semiquincentennial, we want you to continue to dream of our country as a brilliant democracy like none other in the world. There is MUCH to be gained in UNITY! What an opportunity and testimony for the Christian nations of the world! The citizenship of America can demonstrate and experience unity instead of chaos and inequities among its people. Choose to continue to work toward making this happen. Choose to start with defining "self!" Choose to fight poverty and blight. Choose to become more educated. Choose to vote, locally. Choose to show love, even to "those who spite you and say all manner of evil things about you." The Lift Every Voice and Sing lyrics encourages it. Please choose to help unite this great country! What a model for other nations..."ONE NATION UNDER GOD... "!

III. DISCUSSION/LISTENING SESSION: A "SHOUT OUT" AND TRIBUTE TO OUR ANSCESTORS? DISCUSS WHY? WHY NOT?

IV. #3/GROUP ACTIVITIES: (ASK YOUR LEADER FOR HELP IF NEEDED)
SING A PATRIOTIC SONG...REALLY?!?!

A. HUDDLE: Giving in is not an option for the worthy sacrifices made over the centuries by our fore parents. They overcame vicious home attacks, lynching, poverty, unjust laws, and many episodes of racial injustices and extreme violence. Yet, our ancestors maintained faith, hope and resiliency. They knew America could not continue to devalue our race and deem us as sub-human...God's creation?! We had too much to offer as citizens of this country! So, they continued to believe in God, Constitutional laws, and the promises of a fair democracy. You can choose to do so, too. Choose to Believe, vote, and move forward, even if from behind!

B. SPECIAL ACTIVITIES:

Activity 1. GOOGLE Video: KIRK FRANKLIN'S Lift Every Voice and Sing. Listen carefully for discussion to follow.

Activity 2. Identify your group as "GUYS" or "GALS." Sit or stand together, accordingly. Choose a leader (or two) who will be the "guest conductor" for the group. Follow his/her directions. Read/sing each line assigned to you as directed. The opposite group will supply the missing word(s) each time. "All" will read/sing the chorus and the third stanza together while supplying the missing words.

GUYS Sing (GALS supply missing words):
Lift Every Voice and Sing, Till earth and _____ ring,
Ring with the _____ of _____,
Let our _____ rise, high as the _____ skies,
Let it _____ loud as the _____ sea.

ALL:
SING A SONG, FULL OF THE FAITH THAT THE DARK PAST HAS TAUGHT US,
SING A SONG FULL OF THE HOPE THAT THE PRESENT HAS BROUGHT US,
FACING THE RISING SONG, OF OUR NEW DAY BEGUN, LET US MARCH ON TILL VICTORY IS WON!

GALS Sing (GUYS supply missing words):
Stony the road we _____, Bitter the _____ rod,
Felt in the _____ when hope _____ had died,
Yet with a _____ beat, have not our weary _____,
Come to a place _____ which our _____ sighed?

ALL:
WE HAVE COME, OVER A WAY THAT WITH TEARS HAS BEEN WATERED,
WE HAVE COME, TREADING OUR BLOOD THROUGH THE SLAUGHTERED,
OUT FROM A GLOOMY PAST, TILL NOW WE STAND AT LAST,
WHERE THE WHITE GLEAM OF OUR BRIGHT STAR IS CAST!

ALTERNATE LINES: FOLLOW YOUR "CONDUCTOR'S" DIRECTIONS
GUYS: GOD OF OUR WEARY YEARS, GALS: GOD OF OUR SILENT TEARS,
GUYS: THOU WHO HAS BROUGHT US THUS FAR ON THE WAY,
GALS: THOU WHO HAS BY THY MIGHT LED US INTO THE LIGHT,
ALL: KEEP US FOREVER IN THE RIGHT PATH WE PRAY.
GUYS: LEST OUR FEET STRAY FROM THE PLACES OUR GOD WHERE WE MET THEE,
GALS: LEST OUR HEARTS DRUNK WITH THE WINE OF THE WORLD WE FORGET THEE,
ALL: SHAWDOWED BENEATH THY HAND, MAY WE FOREVER STAND,
TRUE TO OUR GOD, TRUE TO OUR OWN NATIVE LAND!

V. #3/DISCUSSION: "SEE IT! FIX IT! DISOWN IT!" TAKEAWAYS!: Your leader will display these selected articles from BUZZFEED, by Morgan Sloss... "Black People Are Sharing The Rules They Follow That Most White People Don't Even Know About, And This Is So Important "(Goodful, Posted on April 27, 2022).

Seminar 3. "No matter how angry you get, you try and remain calm. If you raise your voice even a little regardless of what you say or how you say it you are instantly labeled an 'angry Black woman' and judged wrongly, even when you're right." ____ Anonymous

I Choose to AGREE with this advice! WHY?

_____

_____

I Choose to DISAGREE with this advice! WHY?

_____

_____

I Choose to ABSTAIN at this time! WHY?

_____

_____

CAN YOU SHARE SIMILAR "rules" YOU HAVE IMPLEMENTED PERSONALLY? ADVICE?

_____

_____

GROUP SUMMARY ACTIVITY:

"Our CHOICES for this "American" story are to 1) "see it" (admit it's existence); 2)"fix it" (work to eradicate); or 3) "disown it" (ignore its presence). As faith-based Americans, whose ancestors faced similar or worse adversities, which is your choice? WHY? Write your group's choice and discussion notes on the following page.

Our CHOICE for this story is _____.

Why is this important discussion for Americans who are Believers today? These rules evolve from stereotyping, prejudices, and unfair thoughts about people of color. They are mentally and emotionally stressful for the majority of Black Americans. Yet, they are not likely to go away soon. So, the discussions can provide useful takeaways for peace loving, non-confrontational, and law-abiding citizens. Contrary to racist views, many African Americans still look for positive approaches to solving prolonged injustices in a civil, self-empowering, and faith-based manner. Some of these "rules", if not handled properly, even today, can be life altering or worse. Discuss possible ways we can improve and maintain our freedom loving lives while avoiding more mental and emotional stress. Choose to be proud of the unique heritage of strength, patience, love, dignity, and honor modeled by our ancestors, in the face of adversity. Some of these "rules" were a part of their lives, too. **PREPARE TO SHARE!**

NOTES:

_____

_____

_____

_____

_____

_____

_____

_____

_____

_____

_____

SEMINAR 4. LIFT YOUR VOICE: SOCIETY WRITES YOU OFF... CHOOSE TO WRITE YOURSELF "ON" OR "IN" .... DON'T ALLOW SOMEONE ELSE THE OPPORTUNITY TO DEFINE YOU!

I. INTRODUCTION: Society writes you off? Write yourself in...or on! DON'T ALLOW "HATERS" TO DO IT FOR YOU! It's your choice and chance for a rewarding American experience and story. Our ancestors faced brutal forms of racism in America, but they never gave up on their goals because of it. Most chose to move onward and upward. They were determined to make it to a satisfying place in their lives AND BRING OTHERS ALONG AS WELL! Youth today have so much more to choose from to reach their goals! You can do this, too! It is not always easy. Sometimes it's a very "stormy," "weary," and "stony" journey that we face in these United States of America. However, if one door is closed, choose another one! Don't quit! You have a rich heritage to use as a role model. Research the lives of great Black leaders. Most had to fight some form of racism. But be mindful of our great ancestors' patience, wisdom, faith, and choices despite many obstacles. Choose to be proud! You can!!

II. MOTIVATIONAL MOMENTS: The United States of America's founders were proud of its grandiose and noble intentions, plans, and laws as a rising young model of what a free world could offer. Beautiful ideas were constructed over and over..."We the people," "A government of the people, by the people, for the people...," a Declaration of Independence, Emancipation Proclamation, 13th, 14th, 15th Amendments, etc., clearly designed to be fair, equitable, and unified in the treatment of its citizens regardless of color. BUT these intentions were NEVER fully delivered or equally enforced. They were EMPTY PROMISES. "UNSIGNED CHECKS." They were not enough to penetrate the hearts and will of White America's governing racist body. (Believers remind us that "HEARTS MUST BE CHANGED TO ELIMINATE RACISM..."). These noble works and intentions on paper could not ease or erase the urge to release its ugliest, darkest blemishes... slavery, Jim Crow, peonage, Black Codes, segregation, and other vicious attacks created and directed against its black citizenry. There were many promises made, offered as supreme law of the new nation...they just didn't protect Black Americans. YET, OUR PEOPLE CONTINUED TO MOVE FORWARD, in spite of ruthless discrimination and wicked, hurtful obstacles... similar to some of the ones we face today! BUT REMEMBER, OUR ANCESTORS WERE A STRONG GROUP OF PEOPLE, unlawfully...but necessarily, placed on these shores. We were different in many ways. God chose to make His creation "that a-way." For us, He chose "many beautiful shades of the colors of blackness." We were all created equal to any other...never "1/8th" "½," "1 drop of blood," nor other ignorant racist declarations or rants. Choose to forgive those small minds who want to create, live in, or desire ownership over our lives due to our skin color. God's chosen variety of differences in our multiple facial features, hair textures, and muscular makeup is His Creation, shows HIS wisdom... NOT man's opportunity to muse, use, or be misused by wicked men...So! We can choose to celebrate our differences! We can celebrate our heritage! We encourage you to choose to forgive these wicked evil exaggerations and misdeeds from our past. In many ways, America has grown up and above the need to prejudge, discriminate, and ignore its Black citizenship based on skin color as opposed to character. Choose to read and write your own history! As we approach the Semiquincentennial, vow to FIGHT POVERTY, VOTE, and KNOW THE PARTS OF AMERICA'S HISTORY THAT MUST NOT BE REPEATED! Remember, too, you must never stoop so low that YOU will be guilty of 'Hatin' on another human being due to how GOD created them. You are SO much bigger and better than that!!! Your heritage, even though it included slavery, is BIGGER AND BETTER!!! It is more powerful and pleasing to God! Choose to move forward and never give up hope on our GOD OF AMERICA and His promises to us.

III. DISCUSSION/LISTENING TOPIC: A "SHOUT OUT" AND TRIBUTE TO MY ANSCESTORS? DISCUSS WHY? WHY NOT?

IV. #4/FOLLOW-UP ACTIVITIES (ASK FOR HELP IF NEEDED)
WHEN SOCIETY WRITES YOU OFF, CHOOSE TO WRITE YOURSELF ON!

A. HUDDLE: "Society writes you off...write yourself in...or on!" It's your choice! There will never be a time when everyone will like you or like what you are doing. Set goals you can accomplish and control in your life. Thank God for the many options and opportunities out there. "Cast your 'buckets' where you are..." Take off from there! You cannot avoid racism. But you can choose to rise above it. Keep moving forward! Aren't you better than racist bigots? Listen to the wisdom of "old" people you know who chose to do special things in their lives in spite of the challenges of RACISM. Talk to them. They are everywhere you are... if they have a "drop of Black blood" ...old, young, rich, poor, good character, "not so good" character and others! Each will have a word of caution about racism they have experienced. Choose to continue the fight against it. It is evil and sinful! Choose to never give up!

B. GROUP ACTIVITIES:

Activity 1. GOOGLE Videos: Virtual Performance (300+ Virtual Ryan Mancini) 11:10 min

Activity 2. ELZIE ODOM, Past Mayor, Arlington, Tx, Lift Every Voice and Sing. Listen to become more prepared for a "special performance" of Lift Every Voice and Sing. Ask for individuals who have learned all the lyrics to volunteer to sing the anthem in honor of ex-mayor Odom's video. (He will make this request at the end of his video). PLAN TO SHARE AND DISCUSS WITH PARENTS, GRANDPARENTS, OR A SPECIAL GROUP.

Activity 3. (LONG TERM PROJECT: Date due, TBD) FORM A TEAM. Encourage the participants to plan a project for a juvenile jail facility. Your leader will help you. This visual performance project presentation should be no more than 3 minutes. It can be a:

> dance,
> rap,
> poster drawings,
> and/or other forms of artistic and creative expressions. Together, choose a
> Leader _____
> Assistant Leader _____
> Timekeeper _____
> Other(s) _____
> _____
> Each group will have 3-5 minutes to plan to perform their *entire* final presentation.

Activity 4. (The leader and group will be responsible for suggesting and choosing to perform for a children's group or a special ZOOM audience of youth).

SUGGESTIONS: _____

V. #4/DISCUSSION: "SEE IT! FIX IT! DISOWN IT!" TAKEAWAYS!: Your leader will display these selected articles from BUZZFEED, by Morgan Sloss… "Black People Are Sharing The Rules They Follow That Most White People Don't Even Know About, And This Is So Important "(Goodful, Posted on April 27, 2022).

> **Seminar 4. "As a Black woman in a predominantly white area, I make a point of approaching staff first in stores when I walk in. I ask an innocuous question in a friendly, high-pitched voice, even if I don't need anything. They seem to feel safer around me and do not follow me around when I do that first." _____Anonymous**

I Choose to AGREE with this advice! WHY?

_____

_____

I Choose to DISAGREE with this advice! WHY?

_____

_____

I Choose to ABSTAIN at this time! WHY?

_____

_____

CAN YOU SHARE SIMILAR "rules" YOU HAVE IMPLEMENTED PERSONALLY? ADVICE?

_____

_____

GROUP SUMMARY ACTIVITY:

"Our CHOICES for this "American" story are to 1) "see it" (admit it's existence); 2)"fix it" (work to eradicate); or 3) "disown it" (ignore its presence). As faith-based Americans, whose ancestors faced similar or worse adversities, which is your choice? WHY? Write your group's choice and discussion notes on the following page..

Our CHOICE for this story is _____.

Why is this important discussion for Americans who are Believers today? These rules evolve from stereotyping, prejudices, and unfair thoughts about people of color. They are mentally and emotionally stressful for the majority of Black Americans. Yet, they are not likely to go away soon. So, the discussions can provide useful takeaways for peace loving, non-confrontational, and law-abiding citizens. Contrary to racist views, many African Americans still look for positive approaches to solving prolonged injustices in a civil, self-empowering, and faith-based manner. Some of these "rules", if not handled properly, even today, can be life altering or worse. Discuss possible ways we can improve and maintain our freedom loving lives while avoiding more mental and emotional stress. Choose to be proud of the unique heritage of strength, patience, love, dignity, and honor modeled by our ancestors, in the face of adversity. Some of these "rules" were a part of their lives, too. **PREPARE TO SHARE!**

NOTES:

_____

_____

_____

_____

_____

_____

_____

_____

_____

_____

_____

_____

SEMINAR 5. WHERE IS AMERICA'S INNER LIVING FAITH? ONE NATION UNDER GOD...?!?!

I. INTRODUCTION: A great wise American president, George Washington, stated that "America's duty is to acknowledge the providence of Almighty God, to obey His will, to be grateful for His benefits, and humbly to implore His protection and favor." In this session, we will explore ways our African American forefathers shared in this belief along with trying to make sure you benefited from their sacrifices as well. Choose to take advantage of the opportunities to worship our Heavenly Father and our Almighty God. For African Americans, worshipping freely was not always a "privilege." Choose to be grateful!

II. MOTIVATIONAL MOMENTS: "Blessed is the nation whose God is the Lord." Psalm 33:12. Americans have many reasons to believe our country was founded on Christian principles and beliefs. We are reminded with messages on our coins, paper money, swearing's in, formal documents, etc. Yet, many questions remain as to how many opposing messages of faith have been manifested in our past and our present lives. For example, on Sunday mornings, the 11:00 hour is said to be one of the most segregated times in America. Can Blacks and Whites worship together in unity? A major concern in our nation's consciences, since its inception, has been ignoring racism. It is one of our greatest societal sins, right? So, should we continue to avoid it from the pulpit? Should the clergy (Black and/or White) do a better job in preparing us to show more love for each other while living our daily lives... in our schools, careers, the community? Another profound question by many Christians (and others) since the times of slavery was how did so many White Christians own slaves and support its horrendous, inhumane, existence? Admittedly, some Whites and Blacks attempted to worship together early on. But sermons often encouraged slaves to be obedient to their earthly master's and offered their Biblical justification for Black bondage and servitude. They did not focus on the Creator's love for His creation...regardless of color. Most often, Blacks were seated in separate areas from White worshippers...in the rear or balcony of White churches. However, this was better in many ways than NO worship. Also, in some ways, it was better than the "hush-harbors" our ancestors had become accustomed to using for their places of worship. They were not pleased but continued to worship under these circumstances until they could move ahead. They had to seek permission and support from those Whites in power to build their own...They did. The first African American church in America was organized in Savannah, Georgia, in 1773, under the Reverend George Leile. (Its birth is older than the United States of America which was established in 1776). Here, there was refuge, asylum, solace, and it "was a 'rock' in a weary land." Here, their worship allowed the release of emotions like that of the former "hush-harbors," but without the cloak of secrecy or darkness. Their open emotional expressions through songs, prayers, dance, and praise contained a combination of their spiritual feelings African and European culture passed down through generations. It reflected their life of lived pain, anguish, struggles, and, yet inexplicable joy, peace and praise for the present and hope for a better tomorrow. Their worship was no longer under the scrutiny of their "masters" or "Over seers." Soon afterwards, Reverend Alexander Bettis, a former slave and talented leader, organized over forty Baptist churches between 1865 and 1895. He was not a Harvard Business school graduate. His training and skills were in his DNA! Many others when given opportunities followed his success! Choose to be proud! Bettis, like many others, chose to make a difference. You can choose to do so as well! It is your choice! Choose to help build a better America. Encourage others to do the same as your fore parents! Our Creator would be pleased!

III. DISCUSSION/LISTENING PROJECT: A "SHOUT OUT" AND TRIBUTE TO OUR ANSCESTORS?!? WHY? WHY NOT?

IV. #5/GROUP ACTIVITIES (ASK YOUR LEADER FOR HELP IF NEEDED) WHERE IS AMERICA'S LIVING FAITH: WILL OUR SEMIQUINCENTENNIAL, 2026, SHOW "ONE NATION UNDER GOD"?

A. HUDDLE: Historically, and generally speaking, many Americans have always shown expressions of faith and a belief in God. Early on, verbal and written communications could be seen on coins, Federal buildings doorways, official documents, "swearing ins," etc. Holy scriptures, Psalm 33:12 says, "Blessed is the nation whose God is the Lord." But are we, as Believers, the "light of the world" in the prolonged fight and battles against racism... one of America's greatest sins even today? Could we, as Believers, choose to do more? Did our founders expect more by including God's Holy name often in documents, and special ceremonies? Do we expect more of each other as "woke" young clergy and Believer's in a Christian nation? Why? Why not?

B. SPECIAL GROUP ACTIVITIES:

Activity 1. Google Video: THE BALM IN GILEAD'S CHURCH'S Lift Every Voice and Sing... DISCUSS.

Activity 2. Research: See if a similar video is available from a predominately white or other racial group's church. Write the names and contacts here :

_____

_____

_____

_____

_____

Activity 3. Plan, organize, invite, and/or convene a racially mixed panel of young Believers... (An online version is okay). Invite a versatile group of 4 or 5 youth ministers, counselors, and /or advisors to participate as panelists and participants. Dialogue between the group regarding these suggested topics checked:

a." Is the show of faith, support, leadership, and UNITY among clergy, of all races, for teaching against the sinfulness of racism evident"? _____

b. "Is it a fair statement to make that most young White clergy have taken a back seat to their young Black clergy brothers in the war against racial injustice in America"? _____

c. Is there a "White MLK" in the history of America? Why? Why not? _____

d. What does "One nation, under God with liberty and justice for all" mean to you?

e. The importance of Believers and our democracy... "Our Constitution was made only for a moral and religious people. It is wholly inadequate to the government of any other..." President John Adams, _____

f. Other Faith-Based Concerns for You _____

Activity 4. After listening to the panel, write your "yes or no" opinions here: Discuss.

a) Should we do more as Believers? _____ Why? Why not? _____

b) Should we do less as Believers?" _____ Why? Why not? _____

c) Should young Believers be at the "table" at all? _____ Why? Why not? _____

V. #5/DISCUSSION: "SEE IT! FIX IT! DISOWN IT!" TAKEAWAYS!: Your leader will display these selected articles from BUZZFEED, by Morgan Sloss... "Black People Are Sharing The Rules They Follow That Most White People Don't Even Know About, And This Is So Important "(Goodful, Posted on April 27, 2022).

Seminar 5. "As a Black man, my father taught me, when being pulled over by the police, to pull your insurance and registration out of the glovebox and keep it ready on your seat. That way you do not have to reach in the glovebox when the police are at your window." _____Anonymous

I Choose to AGREE with this advice! WHY?

_____

_____

I Choose to DISAGREE with this advice! WHY?

_____

_____

I Choose to ABSTAIN at this time! WHY?

_____

_____

CAN YOU SHARE SIMILAR "rules" YOU HAVE IMPLEMENTED PERSONALLY? ADVICE?

_____

_____

GROUP SUMMARY ACTIVITY:

"Our CHOICES for this "American" story are to 1) "see it" (admit it's existence); 2)"fix it" (work to eradicate); or 3) "disown it" (ignore its presence). As faith-based Americans, whose ancestors faced similar or worse adversities, which is your choice? WHY? Write your group's choice and discussion notes on the following page.

Our CHOICE for this story is _____.

Why is this important discussion for Americans who are Believers today? These rules evolve from stereotyping, prejudices, and unfair thoughts about people of color. They are mentally and emotionally stressful for the majority of Black Americans. Yet, they are not likely to go away soon. So, the discussions can provide useful takeaways for peace loving, non-confrontational, and law-abiding citizens. Contrary to racist views, many African Americans still look for positive approaches to solving prolonged injustices in a civil, self-empowering, and faith-based manner. Some of these "rules", if not handled properly, even today, can be life altering or worse. Discuss possible ways we can improve and maintain our freedom loving lives while avoiding more mental and emotional stress. Choose to be proud of the unique heritage of strength, patience, love, dignity, and honor modeled by our ancestors, in the face of adversity. Some of these "rules" were a part of their lives, too. **PREPARE TO SHARE!**

NOTES:

_____

_____

_____

_____

_____

_____

_____

_____

_____

_____

_____

_____

SECTION 2.

MINI-SEMINARS 6-10

SEMINAR 6. REVISITING THAT WHICH MUST NOT BE FORGOTTEN: YOUNG VOICES OF HOPE AND FAITH!?! (SEEK DIRECTIONS AND ASSIGNMENTS FROM LEADER FOR THIS SEMINAR)

I. INTRODUCTION: This exercise will offer hope and encouragement to our faith-based African American participants and their friends. As proud descendants, we must not forget or devalue our unique American heritage. Proudly, we will present it as truthfully and factually as we know how. Our purpose is to help show God's love for us amid our circumstances. As African Americans, we honor and hold in reverence our place in America, but we know that there are portions of our history that must NOT be repeated. As Believers, we must continue to fight racism, "rise and build." It's our choice!

II. MOTIVATIONAL MOMENTS: INTRO: Isaiah 1: 17 admonishes us to... "Learn to do good; Seek justice; Reprove the ruthless; Defend the orphan; Plead for the widow." As a citizen of America, and a person of faith, we accept that challenge. VOICE # 1. Always remember, our African American ancestors were subjected to a horrific lifestyle under slavery. Family members were sold at auctions like cattle. Many Black babies were born into slavery and died in slavery. This was our fore parents' way of life for years. VOICE # 2. Yet, our fore parents were blessed in Spirit in spite of these injustices and the brutal discrimination. Many believe, no other race of people could have endured the sacrifices they made. Some have said "Our DNA was designed for the challenges." Our fore parents obviously relied heavily on their faith to keep them going. VOICE # 3. As you visualize, these scenes, realize this system of slavery was embraced by sinful and cruel humans who had no feelings...except they felt they were special and superior. They felt the color of their white skin made them and their race supreme. Slaves, and their dark skin, were NOT even considered human...1/8th as noted. They were only worthy to be subservient to White skinned people. VOICE # 4. But know that this was NOT the America envisioned by freedom loving White Christian Americans who were TRUE BELIEVERS...NO, TRUE BELIEVERS knew that... VOICE #5. All men were created by God. VOICE #6. All men were created in His image...VOICE #7. Christ died for us all... VOICE #8. Black Lives Mattered, too! VOICE #9. Blacks and Whites fought to rid America of this sinful, evil, and inhumane system in early America. Families were split, brothers against brothers; close cousins fought in brutal civil wars against each other. They fought politically on the home front. White abolitionist and sympathizers helped build schools, churches, and notable freedom organizations. Whites and Blacks, together, started the NAACP and other local organizations in an effort to rid America of this heinous system. VOICE # 10. Unfortunately, Whites who chose to fight against slavery were subjected to bullying, lynching and beatings as well. Many white clergy and members, like today, were simply too afraid to speak out or were bullied into remaining silent. But both Black and White Believers remained steadfast in continuing to fight racism and uphold the promises of FREEDOM in America. We can pray for peace in our United States of America. (Spotlight, center stage, heads bowed...)

ALL VOICES: Father, we pray, even now, for forgiveness for America's lack of Godliness in its efforts to build "one nation under God"! We pray, too, for peace and forgiveness for America's many victims who suffered then, and some who suffer now, because of the color of their skin... We pray that we can heal from the scars we have caused each other. We pray to continue to live in Faith and Unity. O LORD, LET A BETTER AMERICA BEGIN WITH MY VOICE. Amen! Amen! Amen!

IV. #6/GROUP ACTIVITIES. (ASK YOUR LEADER FOR HELP IF YOU NEED IT)

WHERE IS YOUR FAITH? IS IT VISIBLE? REVISITING THAT WHICH CAN'T BE FORGOTTEN!

A. HUDDLE: Choose, as Believers, to continue to "Rise and Build." Choose to speak for ownership of the **"idea"** of the United States of America!

B. SPECIAL ACTIVITIES

Activity 1. GOOGLE VIDEO: THREE YOUNG KINGS, Lift Every Voice...DISCUSS
WHO WILL TELL OUR CHILDREN OUR STORY?

Activity 2. The group will prepare to present a MINI-DRAMA/MONOLOGUE for a selected audience. Read LESSON 6 in the session. At least 10 participants will be needed to plan an interactive "staged" audience-participant mini-live video and prayer. The volunteers will be asked to learn the lines at least to the point of taking only a brief look at their script. Encourage the group to select a leader and an assistant. To help organize, write their names on the lines when they agree.

VOLUNTEER LEADER _____

VOLUNTEER ASSISTANT _____

Together, with fellow classmates, prepare to discuss the suggestions as follows:

a) COSTUMES,

_____

_____

b) BACK DROP,

_____

_____

c) MUSIC,

_____

_____

d) SCRIPTURES, QUOTES,

_____

_____

e) OTHER (S)

_____

_____

DISCUSS ALL SUGGESTIONS and INPUT.

ACTIVITY 3. Complete for Discussion. Choose a Yes/ No/ Pass/ response:

a. Do you pray? ___ b. Do you pray often? ___ c. For forgiveness?___ d. To forgive others? ___
e. For safety?___ f. For safety of others? ___ g. For America? ___
h. Other concerns?___ Comment(s): _____

V. #6/DISCUSSION: "SEE IT! FIX IT! DISOWN IT!" TAKEAWAYS!: Your leader will display these selected articles from BUZZFEED, by Morgan Sloss... "Black People Are Sharing The Rules They Follow That Most White People Don't Even Know About, And This Is So Important "(Goodful, Posted on April 27, 2022).

> **Seminar 6.** "I am a Black woman, relatively new to my mostly white neighborhood. When I take a walk for exercise, I always walk in the middle of the street, not too close to houses on either side. I wear reflective gear and avoid staring too closely at any of the houses. I often think of Ahmaud Arbery while I'm walking."
>
> **__Super_Novah**

I Choose to AGREE with this advice! WHY?

_____

_____

I Choose to DISAGREE with this advice! WHY?

_____

_____

I Choose to ABSTAIN at this time! WHY?

_____

_____

CAN YOU SHARE SIMILAR "rules" YOU HAVE IMPLEMENTED PERSONALLY? ADVICE?

_____

_____

GROUP SUMMARY ACTIVITY:

"Our CHOICES for this "American" story are to 1) "see it" (admit it's existence); 2)"fix it" (work to eradicate); or 3) "disown it" (ignore its presence). As faith-based Americans, whose ancestors faced similar or worse adversities, which is your choice? WHY? Write your group's choice and discussion notes on the following page.

Our CHOICE for this story is _____.

Why is this important discussion for Americans who are Believers today? These rules evolve from stereotyping, prejudices, and unfair thoughts about people of color. They are mentally and emotionally stressful for the majority of Black Americans. Yet, they are not likely to go away soon. So, the discussions can provide useful takeaways for peace loving, non-confrontational, and law-abiding citizens. Contrary to racist views, many African Americans still look for positive approaches to solving prolonged injustices in a civil, self-empowering, and faith-based manner. Some of these "rules", if not handled properly, even today, can be life altering or worse. Discuss possible ways we can improve and maintain our freedom loving lives while avoiding more mental and emotional stress. Choose to be proud of the unique heritage of strength, patience, love, dignity, and honor modeled by our ancestors, in the face of adversity. Some of these "rules" were a part of their lives, too. **PREPARE TO SHARE!**

NOTES:

_____

_____

_____

_____

_____

_____

_____

_____

_____

_____

_____

_____

SEMINAR 7. LIFT EVERY VOICE AND SING IS BETTER TOGETHER: E PLURIBUS UNMN!

I. INTRODUCTION: The founders knew that an AMERICA built on UNITY was BETTER. TOGETHER, its people would be stronger, happier and more productive. An America DIVIDIED, as with most things, would surely fail. The conception of America was more than a place, it was an amazing idea. Our ancestors, African Americans, fought at home and abroad to help promote and preserve the ideas of freedom and oneness. Proudly, we participated in every military adventure extended to us to help move our "nation of many," towards "oneness." As we approach the Semiquincentennial, CHOOSE TO BE PROUD for yourself and your ancestors who proudly served this nation as great military men and women. Choose for them!

II. MOTIVATIONAL MOMENTS: The democratic form of freedom selected by our founding government, in 1776, was designed to include all of its citizens. Our ancestors embraced this idea. Most knew no other form of government, except for slavery. It was not a hard choice to make. Our ancestors believed in this philosophy of unity and were willing to help bring it into fruition. They tried continuously to help show the value of making all of America's citizens to become united and free. They fought for the establishment of a new nation "under God with liberty and justice [intended] for all." They fought on the home front, foreign soil, in the air, and "over land and the sea," to make America "a land of the free and the home of the brave" that Americans sang about... Your "daddies," uncles, brothers, and other African American male cousins and ancestors helped America to become triumphant and victorious! (Aunts and sisters were given an opportunity, later...) And, as in all wars, many of our ancestors, along with others, paid the ultimate sacrifice. WE HONOR THEM FOR THAT TODAY! Most veterans were welcomed home as heroes with many privileges, but remember, many of our ancestors were not. Yes, they united with other Americans in the efforts to keep America strong, yet, upon return to our country from wars, their greatest challenges remained the lack of UNITY in the UNITED STATES OF AMERICA. Our ancestors fought, died, engaged in acts of valor, and made many exceptional contributions to this country despite the unequal, unfair, undeserved, unamerican treatment they encountered and endured. They were proud of their roles, once they were allowed in the ARMY, NAVY, MARINES, AIR FORCE, and COAST GUARD. AMERICA'S ENEMIES WERE OUR ENEMIES, or so we thought. But America's enemies (and in some cases, captured war criminals) could dine in places that Black soldiers and veterans could not enter before nor after the wars. The enemy could be lodged in hotels and overnight facilities where our war time ancestors were denied accommodations- -not to mention helped to build and provided most of the kitchen and essential services. Yet, militarily speaking, we participated in every adventure extended to us to help move our country forward. In every war, on the home front and abroad, our ancestors struggled to protect America's interest...Many older African Americans identified with Muhammad Ali's famous quote opposing the Vietnam War. But countless soldiers, just as their forefathers did, made the sacrifice for America, their native land. Choose to be proud! Now, people from all over the world are drawn to the USA out of promises of economic, political, educational, and, yes sometimes, religious opportunities. They know the value of rewards they can receive from hard work, determination, strong values, dreams, and freedom despite inequities. Choose to be proud of your heritage! Our forefathers chose to demonstrate a faith-based patriotic commitment and willingness to move our country forward in UNITY. Out of many one...Color SHOULD not matter!

III. DISCUSSION/LISTENING SESSION: A "SHOUT OUT" AND TRIBUTE TO MY ANSCESTORS? WHY? WHY NOT?

IV. #7/GROUP ACTIVITIES: (ASK FOR HELP IF NEEDED) "BECOMING BITTER IS NOT BEING BETTER, SO WE CHOOSE TO BE BETTER, AND TOGETHER": E PLURIBUS UNMN!

A. HUDDLE: We are the great UNITED STATES OF AMERICA! Like our founding fathers, we choose to be unified as a country. America's friends are our friends. America's enemies are our enemies. Color does not matter. We must continue to fight to be a strong united American democracy. The Semiquincentennial means little if we are a divided nation. Choose to help our country's efforts to stand for "life, liberty, and the pursuit of happiness" for ALL of her people. Out of many, one!

B. SPECIAL ACTIVITIES/DISCUSSION:

Activity 1. GOOGLE VIDEO: The TALISMAN ALUMNI SINGERS, LIFT EVERY VOICE. DISCUSS.

Activity 2. Choose a color from the envelope. Everyone will be assigned a color to match these lines. Sing the melody and lyrics of your color. All will sing the black lines. Make music! TOGETHER! Lift Every Voice! Here are the lyrics.

   ___Lift Every Voice and Sing, Till earth and Heaven ring
   ___Ring with the harmony of Liberty,
   ___Let our rejoicing rise, High as the list'ning skies,
   ___Let it resound loud as the rolling seas,
   ___Sing a song, full of the faith that our dark past has taught us,
   ___Sing a song, full of the hope that the present has brought us,
   ___Facing a rising song, of our new day begun, Let us march on till victory is won!

   ___Stony the road we trod, bitter the chast'ning rod,
   ___Felt in the days when hope unborn had died,
   ___Yet with a steady beat, Have not our weary feet
   ___Come to a place for which our fathers sighed?
   ___We have come, over a way that with tears has been watered,
   ___We have come, treading our path through the blood of the slaughtered,
   ___Out from the gloomy past, Till now we stand at last, Where the white gleam of our bright star is cast.

   ___God of our weary years, God of our silent tears,
   ___Thou who has brought us thus far on the way
   ___Though who has by thou might, led us into the light,
   ___Keep us forever in the right path we pray,
   ___Lest our feet stray from the places, our God where we met Thee

___Lest our hearts drunk with the wine of the world we forget Thee

__Shadowed beneath Thy hand, May we forever stand,

True to our God, True to our Native land.

V. #7/DISCUSSION: "SEE IT! FIX IT! DISOWN IT!" TAKEAWAYS!: Your leader will display these selected articles from BUZZFEED, by Morgan Sloss... "Black People Are Sharing The Rules They Follow That Most White People Don't Even Know About, And This Is So Important "(Goodful, Posted on April 27, 2022).

Seminar 7. "Never EVER put your hands in your pockets while walking around a store. If you don't want to give them a reason to follow you around or call the police, your hands need to be visible at all times." ___ Anonymous

I Choose to AGREE with this advice! WHY?

_____

_____

I Choose to DISAGREE with this advice! WHY?

_____

_____

I Choose to ABSTAIN at this time! WHY?

_____

_____

CAN YOU SHARE SIMILAR "rules" YOU HAVE IMPLEMENTED PERSONALLY? ADVICE?

_____

_____

GROUP SUMMARY ACTIVITY:

"Our CHOICES for this "American" story are to 1) "see it" (admit it's existence); 2)"fix it" (work to eradicate); or 3) "disown it" (ignore its presence). As faith-based Americans, whose ancestors faced similar or worse adversities, which is your choice? WHY? Write your group's choice and discussion notes on the following page.

Our CHOICE for this story is _____.

Why is this important discussion for Americans who are Believers today? These rules evolve from stereotyping, prejudices, and unfair thoughts about people of color. They are mentally and emotionally stressful for the majority of Black Americans. Yet, they are not likely to go away soon. So, the discussions can provide useful takeaways for peace loving, non-confrontational, and law-abiding citizens. Contrary to racist views, many African Americans still look for positive approaches to solving prolonged injustices in a civil, self-empowering, and faith-based manner. Some of these "rules", if not handled properly, even today, can be life altering or worse. Discuss possible ways we can improve and maintain our freedom loving lives while avoiding more mental and emotional stress. Choose to be proud of the unique heritage of strength, patience, love, dignity, and honor modeled by our ancestors, in the face of adversity. Some of these "rules" were a part of their lives, too. **PREPARE TO SHARE!**

NOTES:

_____

_____

_____

_____

_____

_____

_____

_____

_____

_____

_____

_____

SEMINAR 8. LIFT EVERY VOICE AND SING: MAKING EVERY EDUCATIONAL OPPORTUNITY, FORMALLY OR INFORMALLY, COUNT FOR SELF AND AMERICA

I. INTRODUCTION: Literacy enhances life...at home, in school, at work or play. Remember, your educational skills today are still one of your most formidable weapons for fighting the throes of RACISM and POVERTY! Choose to continue, even as your brave and courageous ancestors did, to move forward. Despite your adversities, remember to "Lift, as you climb" and remain focused on your future. Choose to bring other descendants along as well. You can choose wisely and make it count! Choose to continue to build America!

II. MOTIVATIONAL MOMENTS: Slaves were forbidden to read and write. Their owners knew that an educated person was a threat to the evil system of enslavement and the conditions under which the enslaved existed. So, for centuries, education as we know it today did not exist for our people. BUT THINK! Imagine how prosperous early America could have been had they formerly educated as many as they held in bondage! Doctors, scientists, teachers, ministers, inventors, business owners and other talents and skills were wasted while so much effort was spent on trying to control and diminish our humanness. In the process of denying our humanity and intellectual capabilities, America's dignity, respect, and pool of talent and skills were undervalued and lost. Disunity hurts us all! Think of how many good talented White lives were lost in the Civil war battles to keep our ancestors in bondage. It cost over 500,000 lives! Think of the wisdom indigenous people and other people of color who were already on these soon to become American shores possessed. They could have become a helpful part of this growing experiment of our democracy if America had been willing to acknowledge their potential as well. Instead, America chose to devalue the dignity, respect, and worth of people of color. Whites only were allowed to use the great colleges, universities, or learning institutions, though many had been built by our ancestor's hands. For many centuries, they were denied entrance, access to classrooms, libraries, dormitory rooms, and faced other demeaning acts of unkindness and humiliation, just because they were black. Many public schools at the local levels engaged in acts of supremacy as well. Early on, the elementary and high schools were segregated and while appreciated, most were dumping grounds for discards of predominantly White schools. The used-up throw -a- ways that were placed in our "colored schools for our 'colored' children to use" hold many interesting stories. Out of date ragged, faded band uniforms (not necessarily your school colors...), schoolbooks with pages torn or missing, scribblings and doodling's in partially used workbooks, and other signs of "I don't want this anymore, but it should be good enough for y'all..." existed. But remember, our ancestors were resilient, courageous, and "faith-based" strong! They chose to move forward with what they had. We want you to choose to move forward too! We know our country harbors many racist ideas and practices. But it is ours, and we must continue to hope, believe, and fight to help make it better. Choose to know that your education counts for YOU and America! It is a great tool to move you out of poverty and overt racism in the USA. Choose the opportunities offered.

III. DISCUSSION/LISTENING SESSION: A "SHOUT OUT" AND A TRIBUTE TO MY ANSCESTORS?!?! WHY? WHY NOT?

IV. # 8/FOLLOW-UP GROUP ACTIVITIES. (ASK YOUR LEADER FOR HELP WHEN NEEDED) ALLOW EVERY EDUCATIONAL AND LITERACY OPPORTUNITY TO ENRICH YOUR LIFE...It helps to AVOID POVERTY AND RACISM.

A. HUDDLE: Literacy enhances life! Slaves were forbidden to read and write. Their owners knew that an educated person was a threat to the evil system of enslavement. Think positive and imagine how prosperous America could have been had they educated as many as they held in bondage! Doctors, lawyers, scientist, teachers, ministers, inventors, business owners and more help, in addition to the other farm and industrial labor, for our USA! Remember, your education today is still one of your most formidable weapons against racism, bigotry, and poverty! Continue to learn. Rise and choose to help others. Choose to make education a priority. Don't stop with a High School Diploma. Choose more!

B. GROUP ACTIVITIES:

ACTIVITY 1. GOOGLE Video: Lift Every Voice and Sing JARRETT JOHNSON. Discuss.

ACTIVITY 2. For this activity, form 3 groups...1 red, 1 brown, & 1 blue. <u>Read orally each of the lines for your color</u>. Then share and write the next lines that rhymes from memory. All will read the black lines.

1. Lift every voice and sing, _____ ,Ring with the harmonies of liberty;

2. Let our rejoicing rise, _____ , Let it resound loud as the rolling sea,

3. Sing a song full of the faith that the dark _____ , Sing _____ that the present has brought us.

4. Facing the rising sun, _____ Let us march on 'til victory is won.

5. Stony the road we trod, _____ , Felt in the days when hope unborn had died;

6. Yet with a steady beat, _____ , Come to a place for which our fathers sighed?

7. We have come, over a way that with tears have been watered, _____ treading our path through the blood of the slaughtered

8. Out from the gloomy past, _____, where the white gleam of our bright star is cast.

9. God of our weary years, _____ Thou who hast brought us thus far on the way;

10. Thou who hast by Thy might _____ Keep us forever in the path, we pray.

11. Lest our feet stray from the places, our God where we met
Thee, _____drunk with the wine of the world we forget Thee,

12. Shadowed beneath Thy hand, _____, True to our God, true to our native land.

Correct answers_____ X 10 pts =_____Score (may vary)

V. #8/DISCUSSION: "SEE IT! FIX IT! DISOWN IT!" TAKEAWAYS!: Your leader will display these selected articles from BUZZFEED, by Morgan Sloss... "Black People Are Sharing The Rules They Follow That Most White People Don't Even Know About, And This Is So Important "(Goodful, Posted on April 27, 2022).

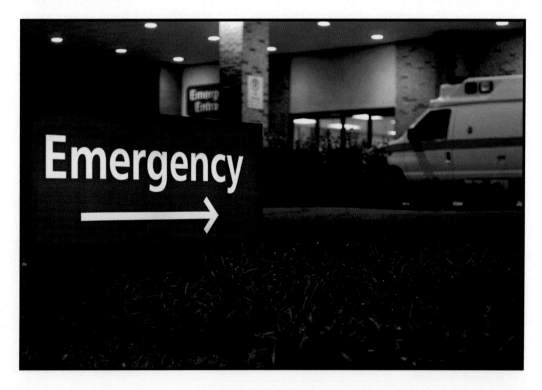

Seminar 8. "As a Black woman, I usually keep my college jacket in the car. If I have to go to the emergency room, I'll receive better treatment if doctors see that I have a higher education." ___eboniw2

I Choose to AGREE with this advice! WHY?

_____

_____

I Choose to DISAGREE with this advice! WHY?

_____

_____

I Choose to ABSTAIN at this time! WHY?

_____

_____

CAN YOU SHARE SIMILAR "rules" YOU HAVE IMPLEMENTED PERSONALLY? ADVICE?

_____

_____

GROUP SUMMARY ACTIVITY:

"Our CHOICES for this "American" story are to 1) "see it" (admit it's existence); 2)"fix it" (work to eradicate); or 3) "disown it" (ignore its presence). As faith-based Americans, whose ancestors faced similar or worse adversities, which is your choice? WHY? Write your group's choice and discussion notes on the following page.

Our CHOICE for this story is _____

Why is this important discussion for Americans who are Believers today? These rules evolve from stereotyping, prejudices, and unfair thoughts about people of color. They are mentally and emotionally stressful for the majority of Black Americans. Yet, they are not likely to go away soon. So, the discussions can provide useful takeaways for peace loving, non-confrontational, and law-abiding citizens. Contrary to racist views, many African Americans still look for positive approaches to solving prolonged injustices in a civil, self-empowering, and faith-based manner. Some of these "rules", if not handled properly, even today, can be life altering or worse. Discuss possible ways we can improve and maintain our freedom loving lives while avoiding more mental and emotional stress. Choose to be proud of the unique heritage of strength, patience, love, dignity, and honor modeled by our ancestors, in the face of adversity. Some of these "rules" were a part of their lives, too. **PREPARE TO SHARE!**

NOTES:_____

_____

_____

_____

_____

_____

_____

_____

_____

_____

_____

_____

_____

SEMINAR 9. LIFT EVERY VOICE AND SING: FINDING OUR PLACE...IT'S OUR CHOICE!

I. INTRODUCTION: Through His infinite wisdom, God placed our courageous and resilient ancestors stolen and kidnapped from African countries in 1619, in America for a reason. Many of us are the Blessed descendants of this chosen race of people. We must choose to be good stewards of His blessings! Be proud! America offers so many opportunities for so many of its citizens. Choose to be "one of those." Don't let anyone harboring their ill-will and prejudices, Black or White, stand in your way. If one door seems closed to your American dreams, find a way through another one. Choose to find you a place of triumph in this great country. As we move toward the Semiquincentennial, choose to be determined to find success...Our ancestors helped to earn a place for you. They contributed countless hours of FREE labor to the growth of this great nation! You can choose to continue to make it work! Choose YOU!

II. MOTIVATIONAL MOMENTS: One of my favorite budding young authors, Rickie Clark, in his book, <u>From Kindergarten To 12th Grade Can = 13 Years A Slave</u>, wrote, "We have a beautiful culture, a unique culture, as African Americans. We come from the oldest people on the planet earth. We've survived the worst crime against humanity in history. We've contributed to the landscape of America via music, art, science, industry, spirituality, linguistics, etc. yet our children have little or no access to the fullness of our story "…. This is a profound statement as we approach the Semiquincentennial. Our African American youth must know their history to appreciate and understand this country today. Other White youth must know the African American's profound, unique, and true place in the story of America as well. To know, appreciate and understand the earned place, of their fellow citizens of color, helps to eliminate one of America's ugliest sins, racism. They must know how the "fullness of our story' helps to contribute to the greatness of America's story. It is an American story, so we can tell it in the same traditional ways of sharing the truth of any past. There is no need to hide, critique, be ashamed, embellish, etc., just be as factual as possible. We are grateful for our special events, yearly celebrations, festivals, etc. but, should a full summary of our story and contributions be shared only as an isolated coincidental portion of American history? YES? NO? MAYBE? African American history that began in 1619 must be taught as an intricate part of American history. The descendants can be proud of the displays of determination, courage, perseverance and importance our fore parents showed during the building of early America. Also, warning signs and forms of entrapment, things to be mindful of that caused us setbacks must be told to learn from mistakes. Some of the laws designed to help us were snares, setbacks, disguised as "helpful." ...i.e., WELFARE, VOTER POLL TAXES, etc. HOW our history is told is important. Stories of personalities, like Jesse Owens, the World Olympian, refuted the beliefs that slaves were 1/8 human, savages, or inferior ...Harriet Tubman was not just an escaped slave, she was brilliant and out witted men on horseback by night without the aid of compasses', etc... The fulness and appreciation for the heroism of many like these must be shared. The whole horrendous and horrific acts of slavery, Jim Crow, and feelings of white supremacy must be understood to avoid repeating. Abraham Lincoln is credited with the saying "As I would not be a slave, So, I would not be a master..."!

III. DISCUSSION/LISTENING SESSION: A "SHOUT OUT" TO MY ANSCESTORS? WHY? WHY NOT?

IV. # 9/FOLLOW-UP GROUP ACTIVITIES (ASK YOUR LEADER FOR HELP IF NEEDED)

A. HUDDLE: Finding your place in America is your choice. Our ancestors paid mightily, but they thrived. As law-abiding, God fearing and faith-based citizens, you have too much self-worth in you! Unlike some racist people believe, you are not a monolithic being. Choose to be an "asset." Choose to enjoy life so much you can reach back and help others! Find a way to give purpose to your life. Don't allow an unjust society to define you, hurt you, or deny the strength and determination in you. Psalm 139:14 "I will give thanks unto Thee, for I am fearfully and wonderfully made, Wonderful are Thy works, And my soul knows it very well. BE PROUD! DEFINE YOURSELF! YOU CAN CHOOSE!

B. GROUP ACTIVITIES:

Activity 1. GOOGLE Video: KITKA CULTURAL HERITAGE CHOIR, Lift Every Voice and SING. Listen and prepare to discuss.

Activity 2. While seated, at random, pull one or two numbers, 1-25, from your leaders' envelope. (Your leader will adjust the numbers needed). When directed, find your numbered place in line, 1-25. (If you had to choose more than one number, line up according to which comes first). While standing in numerical order, take turns to read/sing your line(s). Check your line(s) here if it will help you to remember.

___Lift Every Voice and Sing, Till earth and Heaven ring (1)

___Ring with the harmony of Liberty, (2)

___Let our rejoicing rise, High as the list'ning skies, (3)

___Let it resound loud as the rolling seas, (4)

___Sing a song, full of the faith that our dark past has taught us, (5)

___Sing a song, full of the hope that the present has brought us, (6)

___Facing a rising song, of our new day begun, Let us march on till victory is won! (7)

___Stony the road we trod, bitter the chast'ning rod, (8)

___Felt in the days when hope unborn had died, (9)

___Yet with a steady beat, Have not our weary feet (10)

___Come to a place for which our fathers sighed? (11)

___We have come, over a way that with tears has been watered, (12)

___We have come, treading our path through the blood of the slaughtered, (13)

___Out from the gloomy past, Till now we stand at last, (14)

___Where the white gleam of our bright star is cast. (15)

___God of our weary years, God of our silent tears, (16)

___Thou who has brought us thus far on the way (17)

___Though who has by thou might, led us into the light, (18)

___Keep us forever in the right path we pray, (19)

___Lest our feet stray from the places, our God where we met Thee (20)

___Lest our hearts drunk with the wine of the world we forget Thee (21)

___Shadowed beneath Thy hand, (22)

___May we forever stand, (23)

___True to our God, (24)

___True to our Native land! (25)

V. #9/DISCUSSION: "SEE IT! FIX IT! DISOWN IT!" TAKEAWAYS!: Your leader will display these selected articles from BUZZFEED, by Morgan Sloss… "Black People Are Sharing The Rules They Follow That Most White People Don't Even Know About, And This Is So Important "(Goodful, Posted on April 27, 2022).

Seminar 9. "As a Black man, if there is a white woman in line, you stand back far enough so you cannot touch her by mistake or be accused of touching her."___Anonymous

I Choose to AGREE with this advice! WHY?

_____

_____

I Choose to DISAGREE with this advice! WHY?

_____

_____

I Choose to ABSTAIN at this time! WHY?

_____

_____

CAN YOU SHARE SIMILAR "rules" YOU HAVE IMPLEMENTED PERSONALLY? ADVICE?

_____

_____

GROUP SUMMARY ACTIVITY:

"Our CHOICES for this "American" story are to 1) "see it" (admit it's existence); 2)"fix it" (work to eradicate); or 3) "disown it" (ignore its presence). As faith-based Americans, whose ancestors faced similar or worse adversities, which is your choice? WHY? Write your group's choice and discussion notes on the following page.

Our CHOICE for this story is _____.

Why is this important discussion for Americans who are Believers today? These rules evolve from stereotyping, prejudices, and unfair thoughts about people of color. They are mentally and emotionally stressful for the majority of Black Americans. Yet, they are not likely to go away soon. So, the discussions can provide useful takeaways for peace loving, non-confrontational, law-abiding citizens. Contrary to racist views, many African Americans still look for positive approaches to solving prolonged injustices in a civil, self-empowering, and faith-based manner. Some of these "rules", if not handled properly, even today, can be life altering or worse. Discuss possible ways we can improve and maintain our freedom loving lives while avoiding more mental and emotional stress. Choose to be proud of the unique heritage of strength, patience, love, dignity, and honor modeled by our ancestors, in the face of adversity. Some of these "rules" were a part of their lives, too. **PREPARE TO SHARE!**

NOTES:

_____

_____

_____

_____

_____

_____

_____

_____

_____

_____

_____

_____

_____

SEMINAR 10. I WILL CHOOSE TO HAVE PURPOSE... IT IS MY CHOICE!

I. INTRODUCTIONS: Who likes everybody? Very few people like everybody. Very few people are liked by everybody. Understanding and accepting this fact will help in our pursuit of happiness in a racist society! "I can't change the way I look. I was born with this color and who I am and where I am from. So, the best thing, I could do is to control the controllable, put in the work with my own two hands, and if someone then continues to choose to discriminate against me, well that's on them." People Magazine, Dwayne Johnson 6/28/21. Mr. Johnson doesn't need someone else's acceptance of how God made him. He can be happy and successful "all by himself." It is your choice to help you and your country to become better and do the same.

II. MOTIVATIONAL MOMENTS: "You don't belong here!" "Go back to Africa!," "*(*^%@##(rs, N----------r!," and other such vitriolic words often upset you, right? You become very hurt, uncomfortable, and angry, even if you know they are spoken by ignorant, racists and unhappy people. Why is it so easy to allow this type of language to rattle, demean or belittle you? Why? You can't control another person's thoughts or words...without a lot of discomfort, time consuming, and nonproductive retaliation on both of your sides. Why bother? You can control how you allow yourself to feel about what has been said. Do you feel smaller unacceptable, undervalued, unsafe, unimportant—to whom? White people? All people? Maybe it is because YOU HAVE NOT FULLY ACCEPTED your special place in America! EMBRACE YOUR SPACE! You can choose to ignore or not take such racist rants personal. Such comments usually are from someone who is hurting so badly they want to release their mental pain on you because they don't know what else to do with it. Report it, but most times people in power don't feel your pain and are at a loss for how to medicate. Rise above them! Go high! Research! Study! Know the story of your own unique African American heritage. You will not become offended as quickly, trust me. If THEY KNEW YOUR BLACK HERITAGE, THEY WOULD NOT BE AS EAGER TO try to offend you and HURTLE SUCH BIASED, DEMENTED, INSANE, and RACIST INSULTS AT YOU. Learn your own proud heritage, embrace it, and share it. Choose more important things to lend your voice to. Obviously, their wish is to distract you and you can choose not to let that happen. Choose important things to concentrate on or fight for in America. Voting rights, candidates supporting Civil rights, equal opportunities, job opportunities, poverty, equal protection under the laws... this is much more important than responding to a nit wit. As we approach the Semiquincentennial, choose fights that are worthy of your time. You can you know. The choice to Lift Your Voice is only wise if you are responding to the right requests. Choose wisely. Your ancestors did! You deserve to be proud to belong to a nation your ancestors helped to build! Continue to fight, but sometimes, just consider the source and keep moving forward... It is never easy to ignore the hurt, pain, embarrassment and other ego deflating feelings experienced when you are verbally assaulted racially. However, knowing your heritage can help you to be prepared to dismiss some types of ignorance...since we did not ask to "come over". Many times, a best strategy can be to choose to rise above ignorance. Ignore it!_____

III. DISCUSSION/LISTENING SESSION A "SHOUT OUT" AND A TRIBUTE TO MY ANSCESTORS? WHY? WHY NOT?

IV. #10/FOLLOW-UP GROUP ACTIVITIES. (ASK YOUR LEADER FOR HELP IF NEEDED) CHOOSING NOT TO MAKE YOUR PROBLEMS, WITH ME, MY PROBLEMS.

A. HUDDLE: "I can't change the way I look. I was born with this color, and who I am, and where I am from. So, the best thing I could do is to control the controllable, put in the hard work with my own two hands, and if someone then continues to choose to discriminate against me, well that's on them." Dwyane Johnson, People. 6/28/2021. You can make that choice too! CHOOSE TO CELEBRATE YOU! You can choose to just do it!

B. SPECIAL GROUP ACTIVITIES:

Activity 1. GOOGLE MEN OF MOREHOUSE CHOIR: Lift Every Voice and Sing Video. LISTEN TO PREPARE FOR DISCUSSION.

Activity 2. Choose a partner. Prepare to compete against other sets of participants. Fill in the blanks. See who can finish first with the most correctly spelled answers. (Points may be deducted for misspelled words.) Begin when directed:

(Begin time: min: __ seconds: __).

(1-2) Lift every voice and s_____, Till earth and heaven r_____.

(3) Ring with the harmonies of l_____,

(4-5) Let our rejoicing r_____, High as the lis'tnings_____

(6) Let it r_____ loud as the rolling sea,

(7-9) S_____ a s_____, full of the faith that the dark past has t_____ us,

(10-12) S_____ a s_____, full of the hope that the present has b _____us,

(13-15) Facing the rising s _____of our n_____ day b _____,

(16-18) Let us m_____ on till v _____ is w_____ .

(19-22) S _____ the road we t _____, B_____ the chast'ning r _____,

(23) Felt in the days when h_____ unborn had died;

(24-25) Yet with a s_____ beat, Have not our w _____ feet,

(26) Come to a place for which our f_____ signed?

(27-28) We have come over a way that with t _____has been w _____,

(29-31) We have come, t _____ our path through the b_____ of the slaughtered.

(32-33) Out from the gloomy past, Till now we stand at l _____,

(34) Where the white gleam of our bright star is c_____,

(35-36) God of our w_____years, God of our s_____tears,

(37) Thou who has brought us thus far on the w_____,

(38-39) Thou who has by thy m_____, Led us into the l_____,

(40-41) Keep us f_____ in the right path we p_____.

(42-43)) L_____ our feet s_____ from the places, our God where we met Thee,

(44-45) Lest our h_____drunk with the wine of the world we f_____ Thee,

(46-47) S_____ beneath Thy hand, May we f_____ stand,

(48-50) T_____ to our G_____, TRUE TO OUR NATIVE LAND.

(End Time: min:____seconds: _____).

Correct Answers_____ X 2 pts = _____Score

V. DISCUSSION: "SEE IT! FIX IT! DISOWN IT!" TAKEAWAYS!: Your leader will display these selected articles from BUZZFEED, by Morgan Sloss... "Black People Are Sharing The Rules They Follow That Most White People Don't Even Know About, And This Is So Important "(Goodful, Posted on April 27, 2022).

Seminar 10. "I was taught to be an overachiever because no one expects a Black woman to be smart and well-spoken. I'm not expected to have a voice in anything, and many are shocked when I do. They are astounded when I can verbalize my thoughts and opinions in multi-syllable words. Melanin and ovaries do not cancel out intelligence and reason." ___**Anonymous**

I Choose to AGREE with this advice! WHY?

_____

_____

I Choose to DISAGREE with this advice! WHY?

_____

_____

I Choose to ABSTAIN at this time! WHY?

_____

_____

CAN YOU SHARE SIMILAR "rules" YOU HAVE IMPLEMENTED PERSONALLY? ADVICE?

_____

_____

GROUP SUMMARY ACTIVITY:

"Our CHOICES for this "American" story are to 1) "see it" (admit it's existence); 2)"fix it" (work to eradicate); or 3) "disown it" (ignore its presence). As faith-based Americans, whose ancestors faced similar or worse adversities, which is your choice? WHY? Write your group's choice and discussion notes on the following page.

Our CHOICE for this story is _____.

Why is this important discussion for Americans who are Believers today? These rules evolve from stereotyping, prejudices, and unfair thoughts about people of color. They are mentally and emotionally stressful for the majority of Black Americans. Yet, they are not likely to go away soon. So, the discussions can provide useful takeaways for peace loving, non-confrontational, and law-abiding citizens. Contrary to racist views, many African Americans still look for positive approaches to solving prolonged injustices in a civil, self-empowering, and faith-based manner. Some of these "rules", if not handled properly, even today, can be life altering or worse. Discuss possible ways we can improve and maintain our freedom loving lives while avoiding more mental and emotional stress. Choose to be proud of the unique heritage of strength, patience, love, dignity, and honor modeled by our ancestors, in the face of adversity. Some of these "rules" were a part of their lives, too. **PREPARE TO SHARE!**

NOTES:

_____

_____

_____

_____

_____

_____

_____

_____

_____

_____

_____

_____

SECTION 3.

MINI-SEMINARS 11-15

SEMINAR 11. LIFT EVERY VOICE AND SING: LITERACY READINESS SKILLS, EDUCATIONAL DEGREES, AND CAREER CHOICES

I. INTRODUCTIONS: Education, wealth and political savvy are great equalizers in a racist society. None of these will completely dismiss your chances of racist name calling, taunts, verbal assaults, police brutality, redlining, "sundown town" encounters entirely, but they can greatly improve the odds of being caught up in these vicious embarrassing racist predicaments. However, an education, formally and informally, offers more choices and opportunities in life. It provides more choices and pathways out of POVERTY. You must choose to make it a priority in developing your lifelong strategies and goals as well as diminishing or reducing racist verbal or physical attacks. Choose to obtain as many degrees as possible! Choose a career path that will lead you and your family out of poverty and racism. Choose to help others. Make it your choice to "Lift, as you climb"!!

II. MOTIVATIONAL MOMENTS: A formal education is one of the greatest equalizers, along with wealth, African Americans have in a racist society. Refreshing your basic literacy skills helps you to reach this goal. It's self-empowering! Learning new meanings for words is empowering! Mastering the correct pronunciations and spellings are all empowering skills. Consequently, any time you can spend in learning more in these areas will be time well spent. Our ancestors were robbed of their own native language and forbidden to speak to others who were from the same tribe or group when brought to America. Upon their arrival, many of our ancestors spoke more languages than their masters. Once in America, they were expected to learn English, but only enough for survival and basic forms of communication. Many of our ancestors wanted to learn more. They were not encouraged to gain more language skills nor perfect accurate pronunciations for English. Many Whites did not understand the causes of their broken speech patterns nor the mispronunciations of words. They attributed it to being dumb, ignorant, and hard to learn. Some of the broken English and dialect can be seen and heard in early poetry, prose, music, and plays. Many intelligent and proud Americans, Black and White, love to hear "old Negro spirituals" sung and performed in the dialects of the original scores. An example is, "Bess, you is my woman now" from the Porgy and Bess musical years ago. The amusing and entertaining Amos and Andy show was marred in controversy due to the dialect representative of that time. " Lias, Lias. Bless de Lawd. Don't yo no dis days ab'rod. Effin' you don get up from there you scamp, ders' gon' be troubl' in dis here camp"...Langston Hughes, a successful international African American writer. He often wrote in Black dialect" to preserve the dignity and the beauty of the ordinary life of black people," he stated. Too many of our own people, as well as others, misunderstood the fact that our ancestors were not ignorant or dumb due to this speech pattern. Today, choose the mastery of standard English. It is still of upmost importance. Choose to perform well in this area. Choose to learn English suitable for the many career environments in which you will choose to operate. Use "street" English in that environment. Choose to learn and perfect speech that can help you to move out of POVERTY and advance your career. Choose success driven literacy tools as our fore fathers tried to do.

III. DISCUSSION/LISTENING SESSION: A "SHOUT OUT" AND TRIBUTE TO MY ANSCESTORS? WHY? WHY NOT?

IV. # 11/GROUP ACTIVITIES. (ASK YOUR LEADER FOR HELP IF NEEDED) IN FORMAL OR INFORMAL EDUCATION, KNOWLEDGE IS EMPOWERING...YOU MUST CHOOSE TO MAKE IT A PRIORITY.

A. HUDDLE: Education, along with wealth and political savvy, is one of the greatest equalizers in the pool of weaponry in a racist society. None of these will dismiss you entirely from overt racism, i.e., taunts, verbal assaults, police brutality, redlining, "sundown town" advocates and participants, etc., but it can improve the odds. (Fredrick Douglas, Mary Bethune Cookman and many others were proud examples). In general, African Americans who speak or sound more educated are more acceptable by the majority of people in power. Educational degrees offer more choices and opportunities to escape unhappy people who seek the thrill of hurting others in order to feel good about themselves. Choose to continue formal and informal educational opportunities as a lifelong endeavor. Choose the many benefits it offers. Choose it as a way out of poverty.

B. MORE GROUP ACTIVITIES:

Activity 1. GOOGLE VIDEO: DOTSY ISOM, Lift Every Voice. PREPARE TO DISCUSS

Activity 2. Choose a partner. Together, design a positive marketable #T-shirt slogan or poster message to commemorate the Semiquincentennial. Place your slogan or T-Shirt message here.

_____

_____

_____

Activity 3. Add these thoughts and correct spellings of vocabulary words into your next essay and conversation about your proud African American history. LIST MAY BE REPRODUCED ON SEPARATE PAGE FOR EASE IN HANDLING. Take turns to:

a) Pronounce the group of words below

b) Circle the number of syllables or parts you hear in each word. (This helps improve your spelling and speech).

c) Google and discuss their meanings. For words that allow:

d) Discuss other words that are similar in meaning (synonyms) or opposites in meanings (antonyms). This type of literacy practice improves your vocabulary, speaking, and spelling.

1. American _____
2. United States _____ _____
3. Constitution _____

4. Citizen _____

5. Inequality _____

6. Infrastructure _____

7. Revolution _____

8. Faith _____

9. E Pluribus unmn _____ _____ _____

10. Emancipation _____

11. Slavery_____

12. Segregation _____

13. Massacres _____

14. Reconstruction_____

15. Brutality_____

16. Christianity_____

17. Auctions_____

18. Superiority_____

19. Abolitionist _____

20. Semiquincentennial _____

Correct Answers_____ X 5 pts = _____Score

V. #11/DISCUSSION: "SEE IT! FIX IT! DISOWN IT!" TAKEAWAYS!: Your leader will display these selected articles from BUZZFEED, by Morgan Sloss... "Black People Are Sharing The Rules They Follow That Most White People Don't Even Know About, And This Is So Important "(Goodful, Posted on April 27, 2022).

GROUP SUMMARY ACTIVITY:

"Our CHOICES for this "American" story are to 1) "see it" (admit it's existence); 2)"fix it" (work to eradicate); or 3) "disown it" (ignore its presence). As faith-based Americans, whose ancestors faced similar or worse adversities, which is your choice? WHY? Write your group's choice and discussion notes on the following page.

Seminar 11. "As a Black man, never get into an elevator with a woman alone. Always wait for the next one." ___ Anonymous

I Choose to AGREE with this advice! WHY?

_____

_____

I Choose to DISAGREE with this advice! WHY?

_____

_____

I Choose to ABSTAIN at this time! WHY?

_____

_____

CAN YOU SHARE SIMILAR "rules" YOU HAVE IMPLEMENTED PERSONALLY? ADVICE?

_____

_____

Our CHOICE for this story is _____.

Why is this important discussion for Americans who are Believers today? These rules evolve from stereotyping, prejudices, and unfair thoughts about people of color. They are mentally and emotionally stressful for the majority of Black Americans. Yet, they are not likely to go away soon. So, the discussions can provide useful takeaways for peace loving, non-confrontational, law-abiding citizens. Contrary to racist views, many African Americans still look for positive approaches to solving prolonged injustices in a civil, self-empowering, and faith-based manner. Some of these "rules", if not handled properly, even today, can be life altering or worse. Discuss possible ways we can improve and maintain our freedom loving lives while avoiding more mental and emotional stress. Choose to be proud of the unique heritage of strength, patience, love, dignity, and honor modeled by our ancestors, in the face of adversity. Some of these "rules" were a part of their lives, too. **PREPARE TO SHARE!**

NOTES:

_____

_____

_____

_____

_____

_____

_____

_____

_____

_____

_____

_____

SEMINAR 12. OLD FASHIONED LITERACY & SPELLING BEE SKILLS: FOR LEADERS, YESTERDAY, TODAY, AND TOMORROW!

I. INTRODUCTION: From MacNolia Cox to Zaila Avant-garde, these Black National Spelling Bee champions make us proud! The entire United States of America can be proud of the progress America has made from the era of Cox's "controversial "win, to Avant-garde's championship. The contrast between overt racism faced by the two is cause for celebration! America is moving forward in many ways! She is maturing! Choose to be proud for your country as well as other similar literacy focused events. Our heritage is fraught with innate athletic and entertainment talents. Thank God for such skills and prowess! However, we must choose to expand and acknowledge our many educational and academic talents and skills, also. Choose to continue to fight for freedom, justice, and equality. Choose to fight any forms of racism. Choose to keep moving forward. You can choose America," the idea"! Our determined forefathers did.

II. MOTIVATIONAL MOMENTS: Whether you are in school now or whatever college or career you choose in the future, your literacy skills will be important. Learning to spell correctly is a literacy skill that greatly impacts other skills. It helps with improving your pronunciations, speaking, reading and writing. For decades before White and Black youth were placed in integrated school settings, a different, seemingly, more distinguishable pattern of speech existed amongst Black youth. Most of it was viewed as substandard in much of the same way we viewed our own parents, grandparents, and great-grandparents speech patterns. In segregated settings, most Blacks were accustomed to hearing and using words that were considered broken English, or Black dialect. Most words were not spoken in a clear and/or distinctive manner. When word endings were often omitted or not as pronounced as they could have been, many of our youth (and adults) were considered illiterate. (This line of "reasoning" did not apply to our White brothers and sisters who were speakers of "broken" English, however). Most of us who mastered pronunciation skills were considered more knowledgeable and more educated. Many youths were discouraged in this era of mastery of certain literacy skills and tried to avoid being accused of "sounding White." While many chose to rise above this, in some circles this observation was considered a compliment while in others it was an insult or unappreciated criticism. "Black English was "whut Blacks wuz 'pose to be speakin'! Some well-meaning "authorities" tried to justify this difference with the idea that "thick tongues of the Negro and the thick lips, etc." were the culprits! In other words, our inability to articulate was due to our "Blackness." Research your ancestors, like W.E. B. DuBois, Frederick Douglass, Mary McLeod Bethune-Cookman, Martin Luther King, Barbara Jordan who were only a few of the nation's greatest American orators. Again you will be proud. They were known worldwide for their literary skills as well as their civil rights efforts. Our fore parents were hungry for knowledge and stood out when given an equal opportunity and incentives. In slavery, they were whipped and punished for attempting to sneak and enjoy the experience of decoding words, reading, and writing. You must choose to always have a hunger and an appreciation for knowledge. It is one of the best paths out of POVERTY and offers another excellent tool to fight racism. Education is still extremely important in America, our home---"the land of freedom and the pursuit of happiness!" Many hardworking, goal oriented, civic minded, successful and proud African Americans embrace this idea. Choose to complete as many levels of education as possible. Choose to keep going and bring others along with you. Education and doing your best will never go out of style. Choose to do it!

III. DISCUSSION: A "SHOUT OUT" AND TRIBUTE TO OUR ANSCESTORS? DISCUSS WHY? WHY NOT?

IV. #12/GROUP ACTIVITIES. (ASK YOUR LEADER FOR HELP IF NEEDED) OLD FASHIONED SPELLING/LITERACY SKILLS FOR LEADERS YESTERDAY, TODAY, AND TOMORROW

A. HUDDLE: Choose to make learning literacy skills a lifelong venture. Most of our ancestors worked hard in the fields, mines, and other places needed to advance the infrastructure and building of our country. Few were blessed to enter in the classrooms. Books, supplies, lab equipment, and other necessities were unequally distributed in most school districts for centuries. But many of our ancestors knew the value of an education and continued to fight for access. Many white activist, abolitionist and sympathizers offered encouragement and skills as well. You must choose to take advantage of the path they set before you at every opportunity. Choose to enjoy and seek new knowledge on your own! Learning to spell correctly can impact pronunciations, reading, writing and speaking. Improving literacy skills is never a waste of time! You will use some form of literacy until the day you die! Choose to be the best you can be. Ask any older caring adult! It's what your ancestors wanted for you. It's your choice!

B. GROUP ACTIVITIES:

Activity 1. GOOGLE Video: MUSIC MAKES US: Pearl-Cohn, Lift Every Voice. DISCUSS

Activity 2. Spell the words from Activity 11 here in the first column (A).

Column A (Literacy Skills/Spelling)   Column B (Respelling of Missed Words)

1. _____   _____
2. _____   _____
3. _____   _____
4. _____   _____
5. _____   _____
6. _____   _____
7. _____   _____
8. _____   _____
9. _____   _____
10. _____   _____
11. _____   _____
12. _____   _____

13. _____   _____

14. _____   _____

15. _____   _____

16. _____   _____

17. _____   _____

18. _____   _____

19. _____   _____

20. _____   _____

Activity 3. Check your list for accuracy. Rewrite misspelled words in column (B).

Correct Answers_____ X 5 pts = _____Score

V. #12/DISCUSSION: "SEE IT! FIX IT! DISOWN IT!" TAKEAWAYS!: Your leader will display these selected articles from BUZZFEED, by Morgan Sloss... "Black People Are Sharing The Rules They Follow That Most White People Don't Even Know About, And This Is So Important "(Goodful, Posted on April 27, 2022).

Seminar 12. "Something I know I have to be careful of in public as a person mixed with white and Black) is remembering which parent I'm with and how to act. This is called code-switching. I have to make sure I act okay so I'm not labelled as 'ghetto' with my mom or 'white-washed with my dad." ___ Anonymous

I Choose to AGREE with this advice! WHY?

_____

_____

I Choose to DISAGREE with this advice! WHY?

_____

_____

I Choose to ABSTAIN at this time! WHY?

_____

_____

CAN YOU SHARE SIMILAR "rules" YOU HAVE IMPLEMENTED PERSONALLY? ADVICE?

_____

_____

GROUP SUMMARY ACTIVITY:

"Our CHOICES for this "American" story are to 1) "see it" (admit it's existence); 2)"fix it" (work to eradicate); or 3) "disown it" (ignore its presence). As faith-based Americans, whose ancestors faced similar or worse adversities, which is your choice? WHY? Write your group's choice and discussion notes on the following page.

Our CHOICE for this story is _____.

Why is this important discussion for Americans who are Believers today? These rules evolve from stereotyping, prejudices, and unfair thoughts about people of color. They are mentally and emotionally stressful for the majority of Black Americans. Yet, they are not likely to go away soon. So, the discussions can provide useful takeaways for peace loving, non-confrontational, law-abiding citizens. Contrary to racist views, many African Americans still look for positive approaches to solving prolonged injustices in a civil, self-empowering, and faith-based manner. Some of these "rules", if not handled properly, even today, can be life altering or worse. Discuss possible ways we can improve and maintain our freedom loving lives while avoiding more mental and emotional stress. Choose to be proud of the unique heritage of strength, patience, love, dignity, and honor modeled by our ancestors, in the face of adversity. Some of these "rules" were a part of their lives, too. But they persevered. **PREPARE TO SHARE!**

NOTES:

_____

_____

_____

_____

_____

_____

_____

_____

_____

_____

_____

_____

SEMINAR 13. LET'S HAVE THIS CONVERSATION..." LEST OUR FEET STRAY FROM THE PATH WHERE WE MET THEE, LEST OUR HEARTS, DRUNK WITH THE WINE OF THE WORLD WE FORGET THEE..."

I. INTRODUCTION: We must not become addicted to the sins of the world. The Lift Every Voice and Sing lyrics are warning us of self-entrapment. We can become our "own slave masters"! We become our own enemy. You are NOT free to partake of "the wine of the world" unchecked. Choose to walk away from addictions, violence, destructive ungodly behaviors. These may seem like fun now, but eventually there is delay, destruction, and/or death to lives and dreams. These sinful choices lead to forms of enslavement of your mind... poverty, destruction and heartaches for whole families. Choose to work toward success, independence, and greatness. Even when you think no one else is looking, choose to live wisely. Choose to avoid bitterness and hatred of others, Black or White, due to skin color. Choose to help "yourself" and lift others as you climb. Your ancestors, like Harriet Tubman who chose to risk her life to help others, can be found throughout your history. Choose to be proud of such a CARING ANCESTRY. Choose to proudly carry this legacy forward. Must you hold others back to succeed? Choose better!

II. MOTIVATIONAL MOMENTS: Every hostile, cruel, and heartbreaking experience faced in America cannot be laid at the feet of "mean White folks," "thrill seeking 'kops'", "white privileged," "sundown towners," "KARENS", and other similar factions discussed in private circles. We, as people of color and law-abiding citizens, know and identify with these terms well. Our lives are made miserable by these White supremist personalities, practices, ideologies, and philosophies from the past and many still exist today. However, many tears we have shed, have been at the hands of "Black on Black" criminal activity directed at us or someone we love. The author of these lyrics, Lift Every Voice and Sing, continues to provide wisdom, sagacity, and directions in this song. "Lest we stray from the places where we met Thee-- His teachings," we, too, will inflict great pain upon ourselves. We must unlearn the hostility and emotional trauma we direct toward each other. If we cannot show more LOVE and RESPECT for each other in our own race, we cannot be surprised when others do not! Christ taught the greatest law was to love God, self and fellowmen. It is a mandate from God! "WE ARE OUR BROTHER'S KEEPERS! Where there is love, we will not continuously harm, rape, steal and kill each other. Racism in our society is mentally and emotionally taxing enough! Why do we engage in adding so much pain and destruction toward each other? It has been said that "self-hate many times, causes outward violence or turn our hatred inward." Either way, it is not an asset. We must keep the faith and NOT continue to prey upon each other. Think of the mothers and fathers who have shed many tears because of our own offenses...BLACK ON BLACK crime. Hollywood and TV movies, Hip Hop music, negative images and messages that cause us to glorify and accept violence, gangs, destruction of families, and cause additional struggles for our race is a cycle that must be interrupted. It must be revisited, owned up to, called out, and broken. We must not allow these acts to dictate or define us as a people of color. When we stray from God's teachings and commands, dire consequences impede our progress as a people. We can become so drunk with the "wine of the world," so enticed and bamboozled by worldly things, nothing else matters. Character and seeking God's directions and will for our daily lives is lost in the name of "fun." We become addicted to sin AND WE BECOME OUR OWN SLAVE MASTERS... SHACKLED AND CHAINED! We BECOME OUR OWN ENEMY! Again, down through centuries past and today, our God has been and is there for us. But He expects us to remember to obey His laws and His commands as well. There is great purpose in that! This is the writer's opinion, James Weldon Johnson, in Lift Every Voice and Sing. Choose to continue to fight for freedom and what is right from us and for us!

III. A "SHOUT OUT" AND TRIBUTE TO MY ANSCESTORS? WHY? WHY NOT?

IV. #13/GROUP ACTIVITIES. (LEADERS WILL HELP IF NEEDED) "LEST OUR FEET STRAY...," "LEST OUR HEARTS..." :"TREAT OTHERS LIKE YOU WANT TO BE TREATED"

A. HUDDLE: These lyrics admonishes us as a people of color and followers of Christ's teachings to remain true to our Supreme Being and to our native land! It is reassuring in that He "knows the plans He has for us"! However, there seems to be a dire warning that we, too, have "responsibilities". It is a reminder that we cannot "stray from the path where He leads us." Becoming "drunk with the wine of the world" will hinder us and enslave us in many of the same ways as our ancestors were in bondage! We are not a monolithic race...so if one or two Blacks are guilty of a crime, it is racist and unfair to think all Blacks "do the same thing." Society is guilty of attaching many dark statistics of a few to our entire race. We understand that. But our ancestors would be disappointed, ashamed, and embarrassed by some of our individual and "small group" actions. Let's pray that we can rise above these characterless and sinful displays of hatred for humankind and preying on each other as well...You must choose to walk a path that allows you to keep control over your life and well-being. Also, choose to be judged by YOUR character as individuals, as opposed to someone else's skewed opinions and prejudices. Help others along the way. "Am I my brother's keeper?" Gen 4: 9. Choose to say YES, Lord! YES! Our forefathers led the way! They had to make that choice. So can you. Choose to help yourself and others. CHOOSE TO SHOW YOUR PRIDE AND YOUR CHARACTER!

B. GROUP ACTIVITIES:

Activity 1. GOOGLE Video: HBCU CONCERT CHOIR, ROLAND CENTER, Lift Every Voice and Sing. DISCUSS.

Activity 2. Prioritize social, spiritual, physical, and mental health problems we cast among ourselves that might suggest WE, not racist bigots, are a major part of our hurt and pain in America. It is a major problem for which WE must find a solution. Statistically speaking, here are some major problems that plague our people. Number them in the order of severity against our progress in America (1-15; most to least).

Discuss possible solutions to <u>your</u> first one (or two). HOW? WHY?

_____ Alcohol/Drug Abuse
_____ Worship/Spiritual Degradation
_____ Homicides
_____ Poverty Tolerance Level
_____ Gang Violence
_____ Bullying
_____ Suicide
_____ Voter Apathy
_____ Greed
_____ School Suspensions
_____ Fights
_____ Drop Out
_____ Parental/Family Abandonment
_____ Racial Discriminations/Biases
_____ Other(s)

V. #13/DISCUSSION: "SEE IT! FIX IT! DISOWN IT!" TAKEAWAYS!: Your leader will display the selected articles from BUZZFEED, by Morgan Sloss,"Black People Are Sharing The Rules They Follow That Most White People Don't Even Know About, And This Is So Important "(Goodful, Posted on April 27, 2022).

Seminar 13. "No matter how cold or windy it is, my hood stays off, and my earbuds/headphones stay off my ears." __jojo __Bunny

I Choose to AGREE with this advice! WHY?

_____

_____

I Choose to DISAGREE with this advice! WHY?

_____

_____

I Choose to ABSTAIN at this time! WHY?

_____

_____

CAN YOU SHARE SIMILAR "rules" YOU HAVE IMPLEMENTED PERSONALLY? ADVICE?

_____

_____

GROUP SUMMARY ACTIVITY:

"Our CHOICES for this "American" story are to 1) "see it" (admit it's existence); 2)"fix it" (work to eradicate); or 3) "disown it" (ignore its presence). As faith-based Americans, whose ancestors faced similar or worse adversities, which is your choice? WHY? Write your group's choice and discussion notes on the following page.

Our CHOICE for this story is _____.

Why is this important discussion for Americans who are Believers today? These rules evolve from stereotyping, prejudices, and unfair thoughts about people of color. They are mentally and emotionally stressful for the majority of Black Americans. Yet, they are not likely to go away soon. So, the discussions can provide useful takeaways for peace loving, non-confrontational, law-abiding citizens. Contrary to racist views, many African Americans still look for positive approaches to solving prolonged injustices in a civil, self-empowering, and faith-based manner. Some of these "rules", if not handled properly, even today, can be life altering or worse. Discuss possible ways we can improve and maintain our freedom loving lives while avoiding more mental and emotional stress. Choose to be proud of the unique heritage of strength, patience, love, dignity, and honor modeled by our ancestors, in the face of adversity. Some of these "rules" were a part of their lives, too. But they made it! **PREPARE TO SHARE!**

NOTES:

_____

_____

_____

_____

_____

_____

_____

_____

_____

_____

_____

_____

_____

SEMINAR 14. LIFT EVERY VOICE: "SHADOWED BENEATH THY HAND, MAY WE FOREVER STAND"

I. INTRODUCTION: As responsible law-abiding citizens, most African Americans look for every freedom and opportunity available to other Americans...no more or no less. This generation of African Americans are proud of our many beautiful shades of Blackness, our kinky and curly hair, our array of exaggerated or sharp facial and/or physical features. We celebrate our God's creativity! But our continuous need to remind America of its "unsigned promissory note" is wearisome. An awareness that 'liberty and justice for all'... promised to our ancestors is cause for celebration and assuming responsibilities. With God's help, as we approach the Semiquincentennial, our choice is to continue to help build a better America, from within and without, because it is our home! Choose to commemorate!

II. MOTIVATIONAL MOMENTS: The lyrics in Lift Every Voice and Sing, "admonishes us as a people of color and followers of Christ teachings to remain true to our Supreme Being and to our native land!" We believe God is, ultimately, in control of our destiny in America. Some believe "we were anointed" with a higher power to overcome our unfair circumstances in this "freedom loving country." How else can you explain the survival of our race under such heinous and inhumane conditions for centuries? White supremacy at every level of the government, KKK overt antics and practices locally, statewide, and nationally, did not give Blacks much hope or help for many centuries in eliminating racism. "BUT, GOD!" Slowly, and steadily, OVERT racism improved. Our ancestors endured the lynching, auctioning of family members, and other evils of slavery. Later, our ancestors endured the embarrassing and demeaning "white only" signs, "No colored allowed," separate public waiting rooms, riding on the back of the public transportation vehicles and other hostile visuals of Jim Crow. These were evil and wrong, but COVERT racism, is considerably worse. It is more like other discreet sins that are not as easily detected visually but does immeasurable damage. It can be hidden from the naked eye, but it is usually just as cruel, heart breaking, hurtful, and harmful. It most often goes unpunished or is protected by its own ("unknown to lay people") set of laws. It exists in high places all over America. Covert acts of racism limits citizens of color from enjoying the promises and privileges of "liberty and the pursuit of happiness." It is manifested in its denials of bank business and home loans, trainings in job opportunities, promotions, renting or selling certain properties to people of color, repossessions, higher costs for goods and many, many other sneaky ploys. It is felt in issuing and sentencing, different punishments and judgements for the same crimes in our court systems, planning and preparing paths into prison systems and many other inequities that our ancestors experienced. Now, we must be courageous enough to honor their faith sacrifices as we forge ahead. We are BIGGER and BETTER Through His Grace and Mercy! He has NEVER left us alone. We must NEVER leave Him! As long as we feel we "are shadowed beneath His hand, we will forever stand..." It must be our choice. We can choose to allow God's Holy Spirit to continue to be a balm of protection, direction, and hope. However, as True Believers, we understand we have a duty and a responsibility in our daily lives to help ourselves. We are our brother's keeper as well, so we must always be mindful of others. What, in America today, can stop us from enjoying the freedoms our fore parents longed and sacrificed for us? If God is for us, He is better than the world against us. Choose to celebrate our heritage! Choose to celebrate the legacy of a blessed and proud people.

III. DISCUSSION/LISTENING SESSION: A "SHOUT OUT" AND TRIBUTE TO MY ANSCESTORS? WHY? WHY NOT?

IV. #14/GROUP ACTIVITIES. (ASK LEADER FOR HELP IF NEEDED) "SHADOWED BENEATH THY HAND..." THE Semiquincentennial CELEBRATION IN 2026? 'WHAT DO YOU PEOPLE WANT'?"

A. HUDDLE: Choose to believe that God is in control of our destiny as Americans. Some believe we were "anointed" with the power to overcome our myriad of unfair circumstances in life. Berated, accused of being lazy, seen as savages, and portrayed as less than human...How else can you explain the survival of such a strong proud forgiving people?" Our fore parent's tears, blood, weariness and FREE labor lasted through centuries. Many White abolitionist, Believers and freedom loving American citizens tried to move America towards her goals and promises of justice. But many more abstained. They decline to work towards patriotism and unity. Many of our White American brothers and sisters gained multigenerational wealth during this time. Yet, our ancestors' faith and hope kept them going. Now, you must choose to be as strong, as courageous, as full of faith and determination as those who sacrificed for you. Continue to "rise up and build." Nehemiah 2:17-20. Continue to keep lifting your voices in praise for God's grace, mercy, and deliverance! Continue to pray and seek to make choices to keep you in His will and on a path of righteousness. Continue to CHOOSE to move forward!

B. GROUP ACTIVITIES:

Activity 1. Google Video: NICOLE HEASTON PURPLE ROBE, Lift Every Voice and Sing Virtual Choir. DISCUSS.

Activity 2. Prioritize (1-5, greater-least) <u>what you</u>, as a law-abiding citizen, want from America, your native land. Write a number indicating your priority at the end of each suggestion.

A. Sense of fairness, belonging, and overt acceptance_____

B. Safety, security and full protection under Constitutional laws _____

C. Equal and balanced distribution of protection from law enforcement _____

D. Equal opportunities in educational, financial, job, and residential living spaces_____

E. Voting rights_____

Other(s)

_____

_____

V. #14/DISCUSSION: "SEE IT! FIX IT! DISOWN IT!" TAKEAWAYS!: Your leader will display selected articles from BUZZFEED, by Morgan Sloss, "Black People Are Sharing The Rules They Follow That Most White People Don't Even Know About, And This Is So Important "(Goodful, Posted on April 27, 2022).

Seminar 14. "As a Black woman who works a swing shift, and gets off work at 11:00 pm, I will not take off my badge until I get inside my garage. I need to have a layer of protection to prove I'm not up to no good in case I get pulled over." ___ Anonymous

I Choose to AGREE with this advice! WHY?

_____

_____

I Choose to DISAGREE with this advice! WHY?

_____

_____

I Choose to ABSTAIN at this time! WHY?

_____

_____

CAN YOU SHARE SIMILAR "rules" YOU HAVE IMPLEMENTED PERSONALLY? ADVICE?

_____

_____

GROUP SUMMARY ACTIVITY:

"Our CHOICES for this "American" story are to 1) "see it" (admit it's existence); 2)"fix it" (work to eradicate); or 3) "disown it" (ignore its presence). As faith-based Americans, whose ancestors faced similar or worse adversities, which is your choice? WHY? Write your group's choice and discussion notes on the following page.

Our CHOICE for this story is _____.

Why is this important discussion for Americans who are Believers today? These rules evolve from stereotyping, prejudices, and unfair thoughts about people of color. They are mentally and emotionally stressful for the majority of Black Americans. Yet, they are not likely to go away soon. So, the discussions can provide useful takeaways for peace loving, non-confrontational, law-abiding citizens. Contrary to racist views, many African Americans still look for positive approaches to solving prolonged injustices in a civil, self-empowering, and faith-based manner. Some of these "rules", if not handled properly, even today, can be life altering or worse. Discuss possible ways we can improve and maintain our freedom loving lives while avoiding more mental and emotional stress. Choose to be proud of the unique heritage of strength, patience, love, dignity, and honor modeled by our ancestors, in the face of adversity. Some of these "rules" were a part of their lives, too. But they chose to make it. **PREPARE TO SHARE!**

NOTES:

_____

_____

_____

_____

_____

_____

_____

_____

_____

_____

_____

_____

SEMINAR 15: LIFT EVERY VOICE AND PROUDLY SHARE WHAT IT IS TO BE AN AFRICAN AMERICAN IN AMERICA!

I. INTRODUCTION: Many African American youth of color, and their friends of all races and backgrounds, can embrace and share the lyrics of Lift Every Voice and Sing. It is a song intended to help instill pride, hope and faith in God and a country that seeks to offer equality to all its citizens. Together, tomorrows' American youth must take on this responsibility and challenge. As future leaders and law-abiding citizens, the task before us is holding each other accountable for making America better. Our country is still filled with divisive inimical systemic racism. This is unamerican and unacceptable in a country built on freedom and justice for all. As proud descendants of a rich and unique heritage, with God's help, we choose to continue to work to make America better for all its peoples...NOT JUST US...all its peoples! _____

II. MOTIVATIONAL MOMENTS: EMBRACE YOUR SPACE! LET'S TALK!
"So o o, you mean to tell me that someone down your ancestry line survived being chained to other human bodies for several months in the bottom of a diseased infected ship during the Middle Passage; lost their language, customs and traditions, picked up the English language as best they could while working free of charge from sun up to sun down; they watched babies sold from out of their arms; and women raped by ruthless slave owners...Took names with no {last} names, no birth certificates, no heritage of any kind; braved the Underground Rail Road; survived the Civil War to enter sharecropping; learned to read and write out of sheer determination; faced the burning crosses of the KKK; averted their eyes at the black bodies swinging from ropes hung on trees; fought in World Wars as soldiers to return to America as "boys"; marched in Birmingham, hosed in Selma; jailed in Wilmington; assassinated in Memphis; segregated in the South; ghettoed in the North; ignored in history books; stereotyped in Hollywood;...and in spite of it all, someone in your family line endured every era to make sure you would get here and you receive one rejection, face one obstacle, lose one friend, get overlooked for something, and you want to quit? How dare you entertain the thought! People you will never know survived from generation to generation so you could succeed. Don't you dare let them down. It is NOT in your DNA to quit. Keep On Going"! ___Sharmie Ivery, 1/19/2019, Workshop Notes

"It's our people's story. ...We need to know it 'cause it's important," replied Elijah Pope, 6, at Juneteenth celebration, who came to the event with his mom, Cashondra. ___ Teresa Stepzinski, Florida Times-Union News

"Walk through with strength and pride... It Has Been Earned!" ___Dana Terrell, Workshop participant.

"She called us to step into our tragic inheritance and take the responsibility of repairing it...," Brandon Terry, Harvard University, (comments on Hills We Climb, by Amanda Gordon, delivered at 2020 inauguration).

"I really believe there is a God who looks out for us through all the ' thicks and thins' we go through..." ___ Opal Lee, comments of Retired Educator, Grandmother of Juneteenth

"I'm helping to build, to magnify, to construct, to enlarge, to improve everything that I'm doing amongst my people...and I'm getting the opportunity to indulge in it" __Deion Sanders, Star Telegram, Mac Engel.

"This is my command. Be strong and courageous! Do not tremble or be dismayed, for the Lord your God is with you wherever you go. "___ Joshua 1:9_____

"And I, if I be lifted up from the earth, will draw all men unto Myself." John 12:32

III. A "SHOUT OUT" AND "SHARE TIME" OF A FAVORITE BIBLE VERSE AND/OR QUOTE (AND SOURCE). _____

IV. #15/DISCUSSION/Q and A/UPDATE/TAKEAWAYS: Your leader will display this selected article, The Pastor Darnell Hill's 'Let's Just Make It Home.' The Unwritten Rules Blacks Learn To Navigate Racism in America, Time, June 17, 2020 8:00 AM EDT, by CARA ANTHONY / KAISER HEALTH NEWS.

GROUP SUMMARY ACTIVITY:

"Our CHOICES for this "American" story are to 1) "see it" (admit it's existence); 2)"fix it" (work to eradicate); or 3) "disown it" (ignore its presence). As faith-based Americans, whose ancestors faced similar or worse adversities, which is your choice? WHY? Write your group's choice and discussion notes on the following page.

Seminar 15. "Let's Just Make It Home." The Unwritten Rules Blacks Learn To Navigate Racism in America, photo of Pastor Darnell Hill (Cara Anthony –KHN) TIME

A. "Speak in short sentences. Be clear. Direct but not rude. Stay calm, even if you're shaking inside. Never put your hands in your pockets. Make sure people can always see your hands. Try not to hunch your shoulders. Listen to their directions."...

B. "Don't make any sudden moves. Watch your body language. Don't point your fingers, even if you are mad. Don't clap your hands. Listen. Know the law. But don't say too much. Make eye contact." ...

C. "Let's just make it home, ..." We can deal with what's fair or not fair, what's racial or not racial at a later date." Darnell Hill, Pastor and Mental Health Case worker.

I Choose to AGREE with this advice! WHY?

_____

_____

I Choose to DISAGREE with this advice! WHY?

_____

_____

I Choose to ABSTAIN at this time! WHY?

_____

_____

CAN YOU SHARE SIMILAR "rules" YOU HAVE IMPLEMENTED PERSONALLY? ADVICE?

_____

_____

Our CHOICE for this story is _____.

Why is this important discussion for Americans who are Believers today? It can provide valuable practical takeaways for citizens who are looking for positive faith-based approaches to an unrelenting problem of racism. Some of these situations, if not handled properly, can be life altering or worse. Discuss these words of wisdom from the "old school" gentleman. With your leaders' permission, share with others. Write your notes here. **PREPARE TO SHARE!**

NOTES:

_____

_____

_____

_____

_____

_____

_____

_____

_____

_____

_____

_____

_____

_____

_____

_____

_____

V. #15/GROUP ACTIVITIES **(When directed, begin your written report here on the essay page).**

I, Too, Sing America...Here is why!

Name_____ Date_____ Leader_____

_____

_____

_____

_____

_____

_____

_____

_____

_____

_____

_____

_____

_____

This is MY point of view! _____

APPENDIX: PRE/POST TESTS/TRAINING/INSTRUCTIONAL RESOURCES

I. Optional Pre/Post Surveys/Questionnaire

II. Suggested Videos and Timings

III. Survey/Questionnaire Answer Key

IV. Group Activities Answer Keys

I. LIFT EVERY VOICE AND SING PRE/POST-SURVEY/QUESTIONNAIRE

PRE-SURVEY DIRECTIONS: Please listen and/or read carefully. Each question will be discussed during the presentation of lessons.

Part A

Name: _____ _____ Age: _____ Gender: M__ F__ O__ Grade ___
School_____ Race/Ethnicity: AA__ H__ W__ O __

1. How <u>familiar</u> is this song, Lift Every Voice and Sing, to you already?

a. Very familiar

c. Heard of it somewhere

b. Discussed briefly

d. Never heard of it (stop if d is your answer, consult with leader)

2. Do you <u>know many of the lines</u> of Lift Every Voice and Sing?

a. No

c. one – two verses

b. 1-5 lines

d. all of the verses

3. Do you know the <u>author</u> of the lyrics of this song?

a. No

c. James Weldon Johnson

b. P DIDDY

d. Jesse Jackson

4. Who wrote the <u>music</u> for the lyrics in the song, Lift Every voice and Sing?

a. His teacher

c. his children

b. his sibling

d. he did it himself

5. Do you know <u>the history behind why </u>these verses were written?

a. Give hope

c. Celebrate a Birthday

b. Call out injustices in America

d. all of these

6. <u>Few laws</u> against killings, lynching, and other forms of brutality and atrocities protected these men, women, or their children of color, in the year of the _____ when this song was written!

a. 1600s   c. 1800s

b. 1700s   d. 1900s

7. Does either of these verses use <u>violent words, metaphors and expressions of hatred</u> for America?

a. Verse 1, only   c. Verse 3, only

b. Verse 2, only   d. none of these

8. What do the words in the lyrics of the <u>song offer to youth</u> of today?

a. Hope   c. Faith

b. Sagacity, Wisdom, & Direction   d. All of these

9. Who was the <u>first group to adopt this song</u> as the "Negro National Anthem"?

a. Churches   c. HBCUs

b. Schools   d. NAACP

10. Other question(s) you have about this topic that is not listed here..: (5 Points for asking the question, 10 Points for Q and Your best answer).

Q/A _____

_____**End**

LIFT EVERY VOICE AND SING PRE-SURVEY

OPTIONAL: Lift Every Voice and Sing Pre/Post Survey of "HARD" QUESTIONS (There are NO right or wrong answers... "e" expresses a desire to elaborate).

Part B

Name: _____ ____ Age: ____ Gender: M__ F__ O__ Grade ____
School_____ Race/Ethnicity: AA__ H__ W__ O __

(Choose and/or circle the appropriate letters...Ask your leader for help if needed)

1. Have you ever felt embarrassed because you were (or were with) an African American?

a. Yes

b. Sometimes

c. Often

d. Never

e. _____

2. Have you ever felt scared because you were (or were with) an African American?

a. Yes

b. Sometimes

c. Often times

d. Never

e._____

3. What shames you most studying about your (friend's) African American racial heritage?

a. Images before slavery

b. Slavery

c. Post slavery

d. Neither

e. _____

4. Have you ever felt alone__, left out__, or ignored__ because you were (or you were with) an African American?

a. Yes

b. Sometimes

c. Often

d. Never

e._____

5. Have you ever felt a sense of pride being in a place because you were (with) an African American?

a. Yes

b. Sometimes

c. Often times

d. Never

e. _____

6. Have any caring adults talked to you (or your friends) about taking pride in your African American heritage in the past?

a. Yes

b. Sometimes

c. Often times

d. Never

e. _____

7. What do you (as a friend) consider as the worst part of slavery?

a. Auctioning /selling off family members

b. Not getting paid for labor

c. lynching and beatings

d. all of the above

e. _____

8. What shames you most about today's African American race?

a. Too much crime

b. too little education

c. unsure

d. Nothing

e. _____

9. Why do you think Christian White Americans do not want to discuss the racial injustices they see perpetrated on people of color then___ and now___?

a. Refuse ownership

b. hated it too

c. afraid of reactions from peers

d. uncertain

e._____

10. As a responsible law-abiding AA citizen, what do you (or your friend) feel America owes you?

a. A sense of belonging and acceptance

b. safety, security, protection of laws

c. equal opportunities to avoid poverty

d. All of these

e. _____

End of activity/survey part B (May be used as optional discussion prompts)

II. SUGGESTED VIDEOS TO VIEW AND TIMES

Lesson 1 Jada Holliday, Baylor University Student (3:54 min)

Lesson 2 Oakwood Alumni Choir (4:14 min), Children's Choir Sandy (1:51), Conwell Choir (3:32 min)

Lesson 3 Kirk Franklin, Gospel Singer (2:35 min)

Lesson 4 Elzie Odom, Ex-Mayor of Arlington, Texas (3:35 min)

Lesson 5 Balm In Gilead's Church (4:58 min)

Lesson 6 Three Young Kings, Under 10 Years of Age Performers (2:31 min)

Lesson 7 The Talisman Alumni Singers (7:12 min)

Lesson 8 Jarrett Johnson, APU Chamber Singers (2:47 min)

Lesson 9 Kitka Cultural Heritage Choir (4:50 min)

Lesson 10 Men of Morehouse Choir (2:21 min)

Lesson 11 Dotsy Isom, Performer (4:18 min)

Lesson 12 Music Makes Us, Pearl-Cohn Singers (7:30 min)

Lesson 13 HBCU Concert Choir, Roland Center (6:24 min)

Lesson 14 Nicole Heaster, Purple Robe Group (6:30 min)

Lesson 15 Jada Holliday, "Selfie"

OTHERS _____

_____

_____

_____

III. ANSWER KEYS

PRE/POST SURVEY QUESTIONNAIRE ANSWER KEYS

GROUP ACTIVITY SHEETS ANSWER KEYS

(Lessons 1, 8, 10, 11, & 12)

LIFT EVERY VOICE AND SING PRE/POST-SURVEY/ QUESTIONNAIRE

ANSWERS (in red) KEY

Name: _____ _Age: _____ Gender: M___ F___ O___ Grade ____
School_____ Race/Ethnicity: AA__ Hispanic___ W___ O ___

1. How <u>familiar</u> is this song, Lift Every Voice and Sing, to you already?
a. Very familiar   b. Discussed briefly   c. Heard of it somewhere
d. Never heard of it (stop if d is your answer, consult with leader)

2. Do you <u>know many of the lines</u> of Lift Every Voice and Sing?
a. No   b. 1-5 lines   c. one – two verses   d. all of the verses (ideal answer)

3. Do you know the <u>author</u> of the lyrics of this song?
a. No   b. P DIDDY   c. James Weldon Johnson   d. Jesse Jackson

4. Who wrote the <u>music</u> for the lyrics in the song, Lift Every voice and Sing?
a. His teacher   b. his sibling   c. his children   d. he did it himself

5. Do you know <u>the history behind why</u> these verses were written?
a. Give hope   b. Call out injustices in America   c. Celebrate a Birthday   d. all of these

6. Few laws against killings, lynching, and other forms of brutality and atrocities <u>protected</u> these men, women, or their children, in the year of the _____ when this song was written!
a. 1600s   b. 1700s   c. 1800s   d. 1900s

7. Does either of these verses use <u>violent words, metaphors and expressions of hatred</u> for America?
a. Verse 1, only   b. Verse 2, only   c. Verse 3, only   d. none of these

8. What do the words in the lyrics of the <u>song offer to youth</u> of today?
a. Hope   b. Sagacity, Wisdom, & Direction   c. Faith   d. All of these

9. Who was the <u>first group to adopt this song</u> as the "Negro National Anthem"?
a. Churches   b. Schools   c. HBCUs   d. NAACP

10. Other questions you have about this topic that is not listed here: (5 Points for asking the question, 10 Points for Q and <u>Your</u> best answer). Q/A

IV. GROUP ACTIVITIES ANSWER KEYS

SEMINAR 1 ANSWER KEY

ACTIVITY 2. LIFT EVERY VOICE AND SING...it's MY CHOICE FOR THE Semiquincentennial IN 2026!

___Lift Every Voice and Sing, Till earth and Heaven ring
___Ring with the harmony of Liberty,
___Let our rejoicing rise, High as the list'ning skies,
___Let it resound loud as the rolling seas,
___Sing a song, full of the faith that our dark past has taught us,
___Sing a song, full of the hope that the present has brought us,
___Facing a rising song, of our new day begun, Let us march on till victory is won!

___Stony the road we trod, bitter the chast'ning rod,
___Felt in the days when hope unborn had died,
___Yet with a steady beat, Have not our weary feet
___Come toa a place for which our fathers sighed?
___We have come, over a way that with tears has been watered,
___We have come, treading our path through the blood of the slaughtered,
___Out from the gloomy past, Till now we stand at last, Where the white gleam of our bright star is cast.

___God of our weary years, God of our silent tears,
___Thou who has brought us thus far on the way
___Though who has by thou might, led us into the light,
___Keep us forever in the right path we pray,
___Lest our feet stray from the places, our God where we met Thee
___Lest our hearts drunk with the wine of the world we forget Thee
___Shadowed beneath Thy hand, May we forever stand, True to our God, True to our Native land.

ORAL RESPONSE: Fill in the blanks: Author(s) James Weldon and John Rosamond Johnson, Year written 1899 One major purpose was to give_____HOPE_____.

Research the word, Semiquincentennial. Circle the part that means five (5) or fifty (50).

How old will you be in the year of the 250th celebration? _____ Answers will word, your best friend? _____(Answers will vary)

DISCUSSION/Q and A/ End Activity 1/Lesson 1

1. Till earth and heaven ring,

2. High as the list'ning skies,

3. Sing a song full of the hope that the present has brought us,

4. **Of a new day begun,**

5. Bitter the chastening rod,

6. Have not our weary feet,

7. We have come, treading our path through the blood of the slaughtered,

8. **Where the white gleam of our bright star is cast.**

9. God of our silent tears,

10. Thou who hast brought us thus far on the way;

11. Led us into the light,

12. Keep us forever in the path, we pray,

13. Lest our hearts drunk with the wine of the world we forget Thee

14. **May we forever stand**

15. **True to our God, true to our native land.**

SEMINAR 10 ANSWER KEY

Lesson 10. TEST?! SHOWING WHAT YOU KNOW: USE MEMORIZATION AND/OR WORK WITH SOMEONE ELSE. YOUR LEADER WILL <u>TIME YOU</u> TO SEE WHO FINISHES FIRST… WITH THE MOST CORRECT SPELLINGS AND ANSWERS!

#1…Complete the words needed in the blanks @ 2 points each. 1 point deducted for misspelled words. # 2 Don't worry about the time. We will alert you 1 min before..

(1) Lift every voice and s__ing_____, (2) Till earth and heaven r_ing_____, (3) Ring with the harmonies of l_iberty_____; (4) Let our rejoicing r__ise_____, (5) High as the list'ning s__kies_____, (6) Let it r_esound_____ loud as the rolling sea, (7-9) S__ing_____ a s__ong_____ full of the faith that the dark past has t_aught_ us, (10-12) S_ing_____ a s_ong_____ full of the hope that the present has b_rought_ us, (13-15) Facing the rising s__un___ of our n_ew__ day b__egun_____, (16-18) Let us m__arch_____ on till v__ictory_____ is w__on_____.

(19-20) S__tormy_____ the road we t_rod_____, (21-22) B__itter_____ the chast'ning r__od____ , (23) Felt in the days when hope _____unborn had died; (24) Yet with a s_teady___ beat, (25) Have not our w__eary____ feet, (26) Come to a place for which our f__athers'____ sighed? (27-28) We have come over a way that with tears___ has been w__atered_____, (29-31) We have come, t_reading__ our path through the b_lood_ of the s_laughtered___, (32) Out from the gloomy p_ast_____, (33) Till now we stand at l___ast_____, (34) Where the white gleam of our bright star is c_ast_____.

(35) God of our w__eary___ years, (36) God of our s_ilent_____ tears, (37) Thou who hast brought us thus far on the w_ay____; (38) Thou who hast by Thy m__ight__ (39) Led us into the l__ ight_____, (40-41) Keep us f__orever____ in the path, we p_ray___, (42-43) L_est___ our feet s_tray____ from the places, our God where we met Thee, (44-45) Lest our h_earts__ drunk with the wine of the world we f__orget____ Thee, (46) S_hadowed___ beneath Thy hand, (47) May we forever s__tand_____, (48-50) T_rue_____ to our G_od___, TRUE TO OUR NATIVE LAND.

FORMAL OR INFORMAL EDUCATION AND KNOWLEDGE IS EMPOWERING...YOU MUST CHOOSE TO MAKE IT A PRIORITY.

Activity 3. Add these thoughts and correct spellings of vocabulary words into your next essay and conversation about your proud African American history. Take turns: a) pronouncing the group of words below and

b) circling the number of syllables or parts you hear in each word. (This helps improve your spelling and speech).

d) discuss other words that are similar in meaning (synonyms) or opposites in meanings (antonyms). This type of literacy practice improves your vocabulary, speaking, and spelling.

1. American ___4___
2. United States __3__1
3. Constitution __4__
4. Citizen __3__
5. Inequality ___5__
6. Infrastructure __4__
7. Revolution __4__
8. Faith __1__
9. E Pluribus unmn1_3 _1
10. Emancipation __5__
11. Slavery__3__
12. Segregation _4__
13. Massacres __3__
14. Reconstruction__4_
15. Brutality__4__
16. Christianity_5__
17. Auctions_2__
18. Supremacy__4__
19. Abolitionist __5__
20. Semiquincentennial __7__

C. GROUP ACTIVITIES: (Always ask your leader for help if needed)

(A), when instructed. Respell any incorrect words in column (B).

Column A (Literacy Skills/Spelling)   Column B (Respell Missed Words)

21. _____   _____
22. _____   _____
23. _____   _____
24. _____   _____
25. _____   _____
26. _____   _____
27. _____   _____
28. _____   _____
29. _____   _____
30. _____   _____
31. _____   _____
32. _____   _____
33. _____   _____
34. _____   _____
35. _____   _____
36. _____   _____
37. _____   _____
38. _____   _____
39. _____   _____
40. _____   _____

Activity 3. Check your list for accuracy. Rewrite misspelled words in column (B).

Correct Answers____ X 5 pts = ____Score

TURN YOUR ESSAY IN TO

YOUR LEADER

Blessings!

THE END

Printed in the United States
by Baker & Taylor Publisher Services